Sacred Art
Sacred Earth

by

Heyoka Merrifield

This book is dedicated to the memory of
Grandmother Mahad'yumi.
(Evelyn Eaton)
Go shining, it is finished in beauty.

Rain Bird Publishers Box 135 Inchelium, Washington 99138

©Heyoka Merrifield 1993

ISBN No. 0-945122-01-2

printed in Hong Kong

on recycled paper

ACKNOWLEDGMENTS

I would like to thank all the many people who have helped me with the creation of this book. A blank page is an awesome start to the journey of writing a book and I could not have leaped into that white void without the support of family, friends and the other artists who contributed to Sacred Art Sacred Earth. A few of them are listed below.

Photographers that contributed to the book include the various people who took snapshots throughout the years. Sculpture and jewelry photographs were made by Karl Cordes, Joseph Fresella, Don Hamilton, Robin Krause, Fredrico De Laurentis and CBS Studio. I would like to give a special thanks to Jim Van Gundy and his assistant Barb in Spokane, Washington for the majority of the photographs.

Editorial assistance came from Barbara and Gerry Clow, Katherine Flynn, Thomas Flynn, Snow Deer and Bear Gruwell, George Harrison, Susanne Lanng, Peter Luttichaü, Malidoma Somé, Keith Powell, Sherman Williams and especially Shelby Hammitt.

Thank you to all the models who helped, including Cher, Katherine Flynn, George Hamilton, Olivia and George Harrison, Susan Saint James, Ricki Marin, Lura Miles and also in the family archive photos, Joan, Isis, Ishtar and Astarte.

Book design is by Tim Houck of Lawton Printing in Spokane, with color separations from Spectrum in Portland, Oregon.

("Lord Ganesh" 24 k gold, silver, ivory, opal, rubies, emerald, sapphires, carnelian, amethyst, 1976. In the collection of George Harrison.)

Birth of an Age

The myth of the Phoenix says that at the beginning of a New Age, the phoenix hatches from an egg within a fiery nest. The two phoenix birds on either side of the burning nest are the New Age and its mirror — the former age. The burning nest symbolizes the passing of the old way, and the birth of the new way.

Today, this symbol speaks strongly to us, for we are witnessing the birth of a new cycle — the age when Goddess and the God will come into balance. Many people are saying that the Old Age must be destroyed with earthquakes, floods or other earth cataclysms, as foretold by their prophets. World catastrophes are not the only way that this great change can manifest itself. The cataclysms may well be our personal upheavals as we do the inner work necessary to transmute our old self into the higher potential that is our destiny, so we may be in harmony with this new beginning. The New Age, and the purification of the Old Age, can be a way of touching, sharing and learning to walk in balance with Mother Earth.

(24 k gold, electrum, silver, rubies, crystals,
diamonds, ivory, moonstone, 1985)

BEGINNINGS

I am writing this book for you. As a visual artist, my primary language is that of images. The pictures in this book speak for me about my vision. The art work mirrors myself, the way I see the world and my limited understanding of the cosmos. Since words are not my dominant means of communication, writing is a struggle for me. People often ask me where my inspiration and ideas come from or why I am an artist. I hope I am able to answer these questions for you in my secondary language because I would also like to know.

It would be more comfortable if I never had to explain my work and just let the images speak for me. When we behold a beautiful sunset and something within us goes Ahhh — words can never quite explain what we feel. I strive to create art that has "Ahhh" in it. In my opinion, contemporary art is often meaningless unless it is described with numerous words. This keeps many creations locked in the mind. In my world, art needs to go much deeper than the mind. I will say that I like my art to be from the heart and to have it elicit a feeling, however, this is still not enough. Including the emotional body in the creative process is not the goal — it is the doorway. Through the door of our feelings we have access to the source of all life.

Art that stays in the world of the mind is a wondrous gift that decorates our homes and creates stimulating conversations. Art that touches the source of all that is, gives us food for our soul and may be essential in the survival of humankind. In my early career, I pursued intellectual, linear art; the resulting pieces were very successful. In my later work, I have sought to embrace the Universal; these pieces reflect spirit.

In school and college, my teachers implanted the thought in me that I could not communicate in writing by giving me F's. After flunking English a few times, I forgot about that class and figured out how to survive in academia. I would sign up for twice as many classes as I needed, then drop half of them after the first test. After that I never again had a class that gave an essay test.

With multiple choice tests in my required classes and the high marks in my art classes, I had a B+ grade average by the time I was ready for graduation. When the college computer tried to digest my records, it found that I had never passed the required English class and threw up my transcripts.

The dean seemed much more excited than I was about the whole affair. In the end he did give me a diploma. I think my college degree is still somewhere in a box, as I write this book and wonder how many books my English teachers have published.

The primary audience for this book may well be people who feel like I did as a young artist. There were all my professors who would filibuster about their pet theories of what art was all about. After class, we students would sit in the coffee house and continue the discourse in imitation of our teachers. I developed my own theory of art and could defend it in the debates. The theory worked better in debate than it did when I applied it to the painful revelations of life as an artist. In my middle life, I wonder how this book would have affected me as that young artist.

In order to describe where my work comes from, I will describe parts of my life up to this time. As I have formed the clay of a sculpture with my hands, Nature has sculpted me by my life experiences. These experiences have shaped me and my work, so it is necessary to include them when I talk about the birthing of my art. Often, I have wondered if I became an artist because I was not good at anything else. When I go deep inside, it feels more like art was a raging fire inside me that the world around me or my own mis-adventures could not extinguish.

The fire of creation burns within all of us. Even if we choose not to make art our life work, we must at least learn to honor our creative fire to become a complete human. I have watched in wonder as a young apprentice first feels the power of their sleeping inner artist. These young people may become artists, or just celebrate this newly discovered part of themselves; then continue in another direction with a larger sense of themselves. As a young man, when I felt this fire, art became my primary commitment toward the revelation of my life's passion.

When a young artist asks me about how to develop their career, I look at my own development for the answer. If I have realized any wisdom that my years as an artist have brought to me I would say; "Do not follow fads and styles — follow your heart. When we look inward instead of outward and create from the center of our own life force, our bliss and our passion, the river of life will take us where we need to go."

Several years ago I found a teacher who has helped me to verbalize much that I felt concerning what art has gifted to me. My mentor is Joseph Campbell and I would like to share with you a few words from a talk he gave at the theater of the Open Eye in New York City. "The object becomes esthetically significant when it becomes metaphysically significant, that is, it's holding you to something that speaks past itself, carries the radiance of the transcendent in the field of time. This is what it's all about. That's why art is a sacred thing...The way of the mystic and the way of the artist are very much alike, except that the mystic does not have a craft. The craft holds the artist to the world and the mystic goes off through his psyche into the transcendent."

I ask you to open yourself to the images and words in this book and share my life journey recorded here in my work. As we sit in ceremony for a while, let us celebrate the fire of creation that burns in the center of our circle. I honor the gifts that you bring to the world community and delight in the chance to share with you the gifts that I bring to the wheel of life.

Pyramid Shrine

Pyramid Shrine

Throughout our human family's history, we have used symbols to describe the transcendent powers that are a part of our lives. The earliest examples are small sculptures of the Earth Goddess, associated with household shrines that were made over 30,000 years ago. It belittles our ancestors to say that they worshiped stone images just as we would not want someone to say that we worshiped the written word "God." These wonderfully creative cultures used the figures as we use words—as symbols when describing the mysteries.

The statues were placed on the family's altar and they were the center of attention for honoring the powers of creation. Often there was a flame nearby to celebrate the fire of creation and the smoke was used to clean and bless the home. Many contemporary people still use household altars as the center of their ceremonial life. The altar can be a focus for our mythical world and it enhances our relationship with the mystical powers of the universe. When we look into a majority of the houses in our mythically deprived modern world, the altar for most families seems to be the TV set.

I made this altar shrine honoring the Egyptian Goddess Isis. On the doors are Ra, the falcon, who is sacred to the sun, and Thoth, the ibis, who is sacred to the moon. A small candle illuminates the shrine, in back of the statue. There is a place for incense on the doors to purify the ceremonial space of the person who has this symbol of the Goddess on his altar.

(Silver, carnelian, quartz crystal, alabaster, 1975)

THE SACRED GARDEN
VALLEY OF THE MOON

CHAPTER 2

Nestled in the foothills of Southern California is the Ojai Valley, which in the local Chumash language means "Valley of the Moon." Most of my early childhood memories originate in Ojai. Surrounded by the coastal mountains, this sun baked valley is covered with ancient oak trees which once provided the acorns that were the food staple of the indigenous peoples. Winding its way through the center of the valley, the creek, that was surrounded by Sycamore trees and tules, was my playground.

It was during World War II, and my father was fighting in Italy while my mother worked full time in her own business. The majority of my life was spent with my aunt, who was an artist. Her house was built in 1929, by one of the people in Krishnamurti's spiritual retreat, which is a few blocks away. It is a grand old Spanish mansion that was, and still is, so characteristic of early California architecture. The house was surrounded by acres of elaborate flower gardens encircled by a wrought iron fence.

Ojai 1947

In the center of the grounds was a fish pond with all the creatures and plants that surround such an environment. When I wasn't exploring the garden, I would sit for hours by the pond and observe the microcosm of the small pool. The nurturing embrace of the garden bonded me deeply to nature in a way that still is with me today. When I was not in my garden of paradise, I would watch my aunt paint her landscapes. As she taught me to paint, the artist within me began to awaken.

Our ancient grandparents, before they started to build temples, would go to worship the Creatress/Creator in a sacred grove. The grove would usually surround a spring or a ceremonial tree. This way of touching spirit is not too many generations removed from the world we live in now, and accounts for our love of our gardens, yards and parks. Until my eighth year, this yard in the Valley of the Moon was my sacred garden.

After the war, my father went to college and became a baptist minister. His first church was in East Los Angeles, so he moved my sister, mother and I out of the Ojai valley and into the industrial wastelands. I was thrust into the world of gang warfare, and had to rapidly become street wise. In my gang, the Essexs, we did our best to initiate and transform ourselves from childhood into manhood.

In primitive cultures all over the world, it is recognized that a young girl or boy must be initiated to make the transition from childhood to adulthood. For young girls, this ceremony usually consists of a time of seclusion at the onset of her first moon cycle. She is thought by the tribal grandmothers that she has become a channel for new life within the tribe. This is a celebration and acknowledgement of the change that nature has gifted to a young woman.

For young boys, the change from a dependent child to a self responsible adult is celebrated by a ceremony of death and rebirth. It incorporates a time of ashes, of war, or a time of descent into the abyss and then a triumphant return as a man of the tribe. There is an element of real or perceived danger and pain in the first part of the ceremony. Often there is a scar, tattoo, or circumcision as a reminder of the change from boyhood to manhood. The ceremony is not pleasant and is often drastic in order to help the boys through their transition.

In the initiation ceremony of a West African friend of mine, three young men did not survive the ordeal out of the thirty boys that participated. (After his ceremony, tribal initiation was outlawed by the state athorities as it is in our culture.) The tribal peoples that have kept the traditions of the tribe intact know as our ancestors understood that the initiation is necessary for the health and well being of our communities. The absence of initiation ceremonies, guided by the grandfathers, accounts for a lot of behavior that we act out as young men.

The East L A gang wars of my youth were not about hatred. We were trying to fill a void that was left by the lack of initiation. At the time, it felt like our wars were about territory and about race. Our enemies, the Jaguars, lived in the Village and were mostly Hispanics born in Mexico, while the Hispanics in our gang, lived in Dog Patch and were born in California. I lived in the predominantly white suburban neighborhood in between the other two. In our fights we seemed to be trying to prove to the world that we were men.

I remember the emptiness in my stomach and the sound of breaking bottles to be used as weapons as we Essexs walked toward the Jaguars. The necks of the broken bottles were held in the hands of the ones that did not have a knife, chain, or club. As we swore at one another, flashing our weapons, I was very scared, and at the same time wondering if my girlfriend could see me from the nearby school yard. There were a few blows and minor scratches before someone arrived to break up the fight. I was thankful we had talked around school all week about the showdown. The male school teachers were suddenly there between us, with baseball bats in their hands, before any of us received permanent damage. The rites of passage will happen whether or not it is guided by the older men of the community. Although some young men did not survive in the old traditional ceremonies, many more young men of today do not survive the drugs, alcohol, gang wars and car accidents that have become our unguided initiation ceremonies.

My primary rites of passage came from the dangers I faced on the streets. The welcoming back into the tribe seemed to be the recognition and appreciation from the community of my art work. As with most young men in our culture, my coming into manhood was difficult. Buying my first car was a rite of passage that helped me to cope with my life. Wheels meant freedom, and on the weekends I could escape the suburban jungle and go to the ocean or the mountains.

It was during my teens that I first worked in sculpture and jewelry. I definitely felt a connection with these forms of artistic expression. I have many good memories of this time, and of my supportive family. Still, city life was oppressive to me, and I recall having the fantasy of moving to the wilderness and becoming a mountain man. When I look back on this time, the main priority was to survive and then escape. After finishing high school, I moved out of East L A and I have not returned.

In college, I flunked my first semester as a pre-medical major. In my art minor, I received high marks and this affirmed what I already knew — art was my passion. In a moment of enlightenment (one that probably saved my life) I decided to make art my life focus. We all come to this crossroad at some point in our life; in the choices we make, we must follow our heart.

While doing graduate work in college, I became attracted to hiking and renewed my childhood desire to enter into Nature's wilderness. Simultaneously, my art career was in full swing. The national art magazines had started to notice my work in the L A galleries and I had just completed my first show at an art museum. My work was showing the influences of the contemporary art that I had been exposed to in college. The encouraging successes of my sculpture and jewelry pieces at a young age left me somehow empty and I knew that something was missing. Art seemed to be treated as a product to be bought and sold. Most art, including my own, seemed egocentric and intellectual. The ancient pieces I had studied in my art history classes had a power that was missing from most modern work.

I became disillusioned with being an artist because I wanted my life to have a higher purpose than becoming rich or famous or an expert in my art. I remember being at a cocktail party at my gallery owner's house with many of our art patrons in attendance. While talking to a client about purchasing one of my sculptures, I stepped out of myself and viewed the two of us as if from across the room. If this was what being an artist was all about, I realized that I did not want to be an artist.

It was in the mid-sixties and several close friends asked me to join them in forming a community called the Garden of Spring, in a wilderness area of Mt. Palomar. Aspiring to find what was lacking in my life, I walked away from my graduate program and my art career. When I arrived at the cabin, I discovered that my friends had changed their mind and moved to Haight Ashbury in San Francisco, and I found myself living alone in the wilderness. I had always fantasized about testing myself by living alone in the wild, so I stayed.

HAIGHT ASHBURY 1966

DANCING INDIAN

This wood sculpture is the only piece that has survived from the few works I did in high school. I knew from an early age that I was happiest when doing something artistic with my hands although this sculpture made me wonder if art might be my life's work. It was entered into a national high school competition in New York and won first place in its category.

(Ash wood, 30 inches, 1958)

Pegasus

While in college my passion was awakened when the sculpture Muse spoke to me. I made a series of mythological pieces by forging and welding steel sheet. They were elongated and rather anguished looking while they seemed to be saying that the contemporary archetypal powers were not as powerful as in ancient times.

(Welded steel, 50 inches, 1965)

Arc de Triomphe

The monumental pieces in my Santa Barbara museum show are from 1966 when I was very caught up in protesting the war in Viet Nam. The Arc de Triomphe and the Monolith speak about the carnage of war — not the glory of war.

("Arc de Triomphe," plastics, 9 feet, 1966

"Monolith," plastics, 12 feet, 1966

"Icon," bronze 12 inches, 1966)

16

EDWARD MERRIFIELD

SCULPTURES AT THE SANTA BARBARA MUSEUM OF ART
MARCH 9 – APRIL 16, – OPENING MARCH 11, 3 – 5:00 P.M.

SANTA BARBARA 1966

17

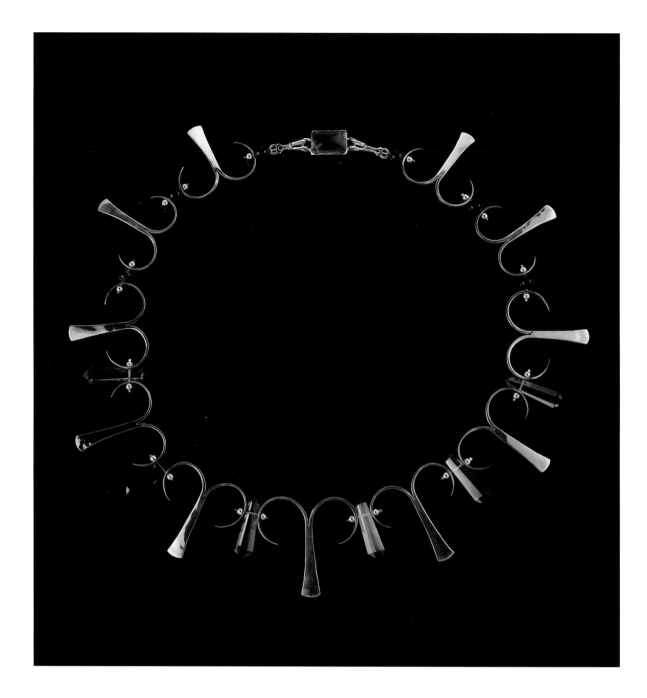

FORGED NECKLACE

This was one of the first necklaces that I made in college. The technique that I used was that of forging silver wire, and the style reflects the contemporary style of my jewelry master, Arline Fisch.

(Silver, smokey quartz, 1963)

THE GARDEN OF SPRING
EMBRACING A MYTH

F or a year, I lived alone at the Garden of Spring with the wild inhabitants of the area, plus a few chickens, a milk goat, a cat, a dog and a garden. Surrounded by this natural environment, I started to feel the natural rhythms of Nature and to have a better understanding of my place within the cycles of life around me.

There was time for me to explore the many spiritual disciplines that are a part of our global human family. Within each discipline there was a myth that tried to explain the mystery of the transcendent. In their essence, it seemed to me that our myths held more similarities than they did conflicts. The shamanistic teachings of the Native American peoples spoke especially strongly to me. The ancient tribal way of relating to the universe resonated with my part-Indian ancestry and with the fact that the Native Americans are the keepers of the mythology of the continent I was born upon.

In my quest for wholeness, I studied the teachings of many of our wise grandparents. Within every religion and mythology there were hidden gems of wisdom about life. After much study, I concluded that we can follow the ways of any of our great teachers to find our unique potential, or we may learn from their teacher — Nature.

The difficulty with following the way of any teachers is that it is difficult for them to communicate to us their inner experiences. Words spoken by our teachers have slightly different meanings to us, often because the teachings have gone through many translations. Written or spoken language speaks primarily to our intellect and is not easily understood by our body, our emotions or our spirit. For this reason, most of our teachers used mythology, symbolism and allegory as their teaching tools. They knew that, in this way, their medicine stories would affect us on many levels, not just intellectually.

Our Grandparents received their understanding of life through observing Nature. Reflected in Nature we see our spiritual parents, Creatress and Creator. When our teachers wanted to connect with Divinity, they went alone into the wilderness. In the natural environment, they could feel the rhythms and cycles of the Earth. Everything was a part of the Goddess/God and had something to teach them.

In our families and communities, we tend to see the world as segregated between "myself" and "other." From the perspective of "I," our ego can separate us from the greater "I" of Nature: All That Is. We have much to learn from our family and community, although it often cuts us off from what we are meant to learn from Nature. In Nature, the animals, the weather, the elements, the seasons, the trees, everything forms a pattern and that pattern is Her language. If we move to another country we begin to learn the language of the people living there and if we live close to Nature we will learn Her language as she speaks to us. If we can come to understand her oracle, we will share in the infinite wisdom of this teacher.

As I lived close to the land, I began to learn the language of the Earth. This time alone became for me a visionquest, even though there was not the traditional guidance from the elders of a tribe. I came to view this period as a time of rites of passage, seeking understanding from the universe. It changed forever my perspective of the world. I was able to experience an interrelationship with all life. In my new image plants, animals, minerals, elementals, spirits and humans were all related and interdependent.

THE GODDESS

During this time, I learned about the Goddess. This subject was definitely left out of my childhood education and the more I read on the subject the more I realized the importance of this concept. In college, I had studied Zen Buddhism and meditation had become an integral part of my life. I continued this practice on the mountain, each day taking my goat to the stream to graze while I sat for awhile. By becoming more integrated with Nature, I soon realized that I was meditating in a deeper and more connected way than I had experienced so far. As I became more connected to Nature I experienced a depth of my soul that I had not touched before, and I realized that this epiphany was my bonding with the Earth Mother. After this realization, I followed the example of the Native Americans and included the Goddess in my prayers to the Creator.

On my daily walks in the woods, I realized that more and more, the plants and animals were accepting me as part of their circle. Once when I was sitting in a small cave, a coyote looked in at me only a few feet away. Another time, the great horned owl that lived on the land, let me approach within ten feet of her. She held me in her gaze with direct eye contact.

There seemed to be something that she was communicating to me. As I tried to understand what she wanted to reveal, her eyes broke contact with mine and she looked at my feet. When I followed her gaze I saw that she had left me one of her feathers.

As a child, I had no tribal elders to teach me about a sweet medicine gift, and what a power animal may give away to a human. Sometimes this gift can be a meeting with an animal at an auspicious time like during a vision quest and there are times when a gift may be received, as in this encounter with the owl. Much later, I learned that in the native tradition, a feather like this is put into a medicine bundle, and an offering of some sort, often tobacco, is left for the animal. A medicine bundle is a collection of sacred objects, like the ceremonial "peace" pipe, that are used in ceremony. At the time, I did feel that this event was special and put the feather in my hat. I wish that I still had this feather for my medicine bundle which includes similar paraphernalia. Years later, my hat was in the Gypsy wagon along with another medicine animal power, my part coyote dog Argos, and he ate both the hat and the give-a-way feather.

This meeting with the owl and similar events in my outer life were bringing about a change in my inner self. When I began to do my art work again, these inner changes would modify my work intensely. My art work would reflect the changes in the way I viewed life. The new pieces would mirror the relationships I was learning from Nature. This new perspective of the way I related to the world would be closer to the artists of the Lascaux Caves in France than to the modern artists. These paintings are rendered in exquisite artistic detail and the animals were painted with a radiant life.

These ancient grandparents left us our oldest example of the art of painting in the caves of Europe. Our artistic ancestors were the shamans of the tribes who took the young people into the caves for initiation and ceremony. Caves are doorways into the womb of our Mother Earth, and after a frightening journey in complete darkness into the body of the Great Mother, the medicine person would light a fire. Painted on the walls and ceiling of the cave would appear the animal powers on which the tribe depended for their survival.

After experiencing fear in the journey into the underworld, and the awe from viewing the incredible paintings, the young people were in a receptive vein to receive the lessons of their spiritual teachers. We have only to feel the power and spirit radiating from the cave art to know that the teachings spoke of an honoring and interdependent relationship with the animal powers. After 30,000 years, the paintings may still speak to us of learning a balance with Nature that is important to us today. When we view these early works of art, we can feel the loss of a connection that those painters had with life. After becoming more connected with nature, I knew that I wanted to continue making art, only now I wanted to work from the perspective of these ancient shamans.

After this time alone in the wilderness, I have continued to set aside time for visionquest. In a ceremonial time of contemplation I strive to regain the perspective of the ancient shaman artists. I will step outside the world of demands and obligations to feel the natural flow of Nature and experience who I am. This visionquest time has become such a part of me, that when I get too busy and neglect to take time off, the universe gifts me by thrusting me into times of solitude.

THE GYPSY TINKER

In the last month of my stay at the Garden of Spring, my hermitage ended. It was a very colorful and open period, and I invited a few of my hippie friends to stay with me. They in turn had a few friends and soon I was living in a communal family of about ten people that could grow to thirty or forty on the weekends. One weekend we went to a crafts fair called the Renaissance Pleasure Fair where most people came dressed in period costumes. It was held in the oak-covered, rolling hills north of Los Angeles. Dressed in appropriate costumes, which were not too different from the clothes we normally wore in the early 60's, we snuck in around the ticket gate. Walking down the hill to a colorful Gypsy camp of flowing banners, ancient and ethnic music, dancers, jugglers, Shakespearean actors, and booths selling crafts, I knew I had found a new home.

It was in the first anarchistic years of what was to become very structured and the most established arts and crafts fair in America. The Renaissance Fair had a very humble beginning with simple hand made crafts that were a reaction to the mass produced objects that had become the norm in our lives. After several years, the craftspeople at the fair, including myself, experienced a true Renaissance of the arts being birthed in California. Hand blown glass, ethnic dance and music, jewelry, ancient theater, stained glass, and many other ancient arts reawakened with a new life.

The real fun began after the close of the fair to the public each night. We would camp out and live at the fair grounds for the month of the fair. Each night there would be campfires, music, and dancing in what became a wonderful Gypsy camp. Twice a year we would meet at the fair to renew friendships, relationships, and to see the new work we were all creating.

In that year of living alone at the Garden of Spring, I felt very content with the simple life I had established. If I continued, I could see my life laid

RENAISSANCE FAIR 1967

out before me and it appeared to be a good life. Still, I felt there was more that I was meant to experience than the life of an artistic hermit monk and sometimes Gypsy tinker. I wanted the joy of being in a family. This desire manifested the commune and soon a family. One weekend, a friend picked up some hitchhikers bound for another destination and brought them to the land. One of them was Joan, the woman I would marry and share my life with for the next fourteen years. We had three daughters whom we named after different aspects of the Goddess: Isis, Ishtar and Astarte.

AIRCRAFT MONUMENT

This show at Orlando Gallery was to be my last sculpture exhibit for several years. After the show, I gave away the pieces that had not sold before we moved north to Washington. My friend next door, a Mexican landscaper, was thrilled when he received the piece I am sitting on. I wonder now what he thought about it and if it is still standing in his yard.

("Aircraft Monument" aluminum, 14 feet, 1967

"Universal Icon" bronze, 6 feet, 1966 "Totem," bronze, 36 inches, 1966)

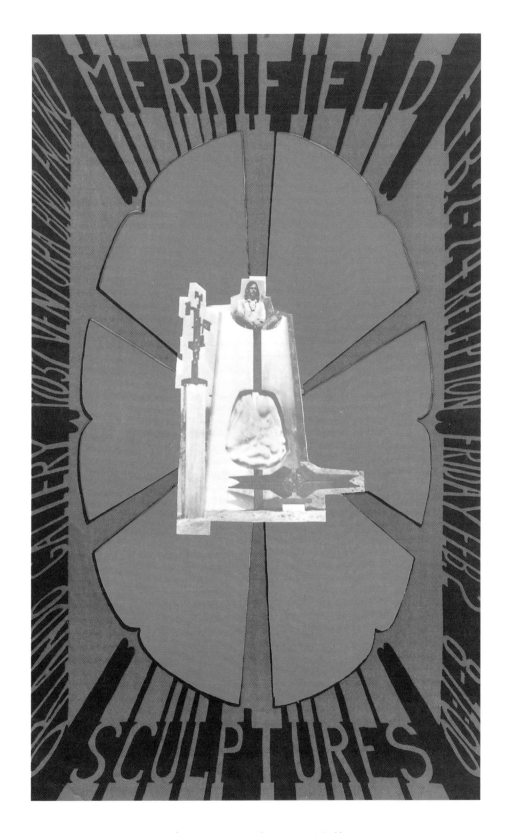

GARDEN OF SPRING 1967

CROW SHIELD

The carrion-eating crow became northern Europe's common symbol of the death-goddess. Her Valkyries, sometimes called Crows, cradle heroes as they fly them to Valhalla. The word crow comes from the Goddess Rea Kronia (Coronis), Mother Time, who brings the gift of the Great Changer to all. The Native Americans call the crows, "little black eagles." They are the law birds, representing the circle of natural law.

(24 k gold, silver, black opal, sapphires, 1975
In the collection of Joni Mitchell.)

Isis

Isis was the principal goddess of Egypt and was worshipped throughout the Greco-Roman world. One of Isis' many titles is the Golden Cow wetnurse to the human race and mother to the Golden Calf, Horus. She was the first personification of the Goddess that I personally worked with. Later, White Buffalo Woman of the Native American tradition, became part of my personal mythology of the Goddess.

For me these two goddess have merged into one that celebrates my genetic memory of Europe and America. This statue of White Buffalo Isis, stands on my altar as a doorway through which I can touch the radiance of the Great Goddess. As with any mythological icon, this sculpture is only a representation of the transcendent power that it symbolizes.

Much of the mythology of Isis, Osiris and Horus was adopted by Christianity. It is written that Jesus went to Egypt as a young boy and he must have studied in the temples of Isis for the root of his name is hidden within the name of Isis. Also his mother, the Virgin Mary, absorbed much of the iconography and the widespread worship of Isis. Some of the early Christians in Rome called themselves Pastophori [pastors] which meant "shepherds" or "servants of Isis."

To her worshipers, Isis was known as the goddess of wisdom. She instructed humankind in the mysteries of life. The hieroglyphs on the base of the sculpture read "May I be joined with Isis, the Divine Mother." Soon after I finished this statue, CBS approached me to include my work on what was at that time their most widely viewed special in history. On the "Treasures of Tutankhamen" special, I read what was inscribed on the door to Isis' ancient temple as this sculpture was projected into millions of homes: "I, Isis am all that has been, that is or shall be; no mortal man hath ever me unveiled."

(Bronze, silver, 24 k gold, emeralds, crystal, ivory,
osprey feather, seed beads, 1975)

on page 28

MERRY FIELD MEADOWS
THE NORTH COUNTRY

Onto the back of my pickup truck I built a Gypsy wagon for us to live in. On a trip to Alaska, we only got as far as the Pacific Northwest and found a place to park our Gypsy wagon for several years. Our new home, which we called Merry Field Meadows, was on an Indian reservation. It was very remote and a wild pristine wilderness . Miles from our nearest neighbor, bears, deer, coyotes and eagles were frequent visitors to our farm. Creating our dream of living off the land, we were able to live like our pioneer ancestors. We built our home, dug a well, raised most of our food and managed without electricity.

MERRY FIELD MEADOWS 1970

For the next decade, we traveled around in our Gypsy wagon between Northeast Washington and California, and sold our work at the Renaissance fairs. At home we worked in the garden, on our house or with our crafts. We were making hand crafted clothes, jewelry and musical instruments to sell at the fairs.

I will have to admit that during the sixties and seventies, drugs were a part of our life. My initial reaction to the varous substances that were available at this time was that it seemed like they caused an expansion into places I was beginning to reach through meditation — also it was a fun way to party. Later, after years of experimentation with various mind altering substances, I came to the conclusion that for every inner door that drugs seemed to open there was also a door that they closed. For every person who was able to expand their consciousness in a way that was empowering or enlightening, I saw a multitude of people who lost their soul to dependance and addiction. It felt like abusing drugs was playing Russian Roulette with only one empty chamber — the odds were not good and the game was deadly.

Also, I realized that by my using drugs I was validating something to my children and my friends that might destroy them. Before a sundance, my chief told me how he had given up alcohol when he became a medicine person because the children looked to him as an example of how to live their life. Grandmother Eaton, before she crossed over, had suggested a ceremony to end the relationship that I had formed with drugs. Remembering her words, I carried my little bag of peyote, marijuana, LSD, mushrooms, etc. to a mountain top, and sat in ceremony. I thanked the substances for all the lessons they had given to me and asked the assembled forces to help my friends who were held captive by various addictions. I saw that drugs were not the only addictions in life. Any power, which may even include a person's religion, may block the center of our own life force from expression. My own addiction of workaholism had defiantly shut out certain aspects of myself, and the way I approached work needed to be balanced. I dug a hole in the ground and placing the substances inside, they were given back to the Earth. My grandmother was not with me, although her spirit came to the ceremony. Her animal power, a red tailed hawk, circled above my head singing as I walked to the mountain and during the entire ceremony.

MUSIC MUSE

Part of our passion at this time was very much centered around music. The music we played nightly is hard to define; it had a striking resemblance to what is now called New Age music. The music we created and the instruments we used were influenced by Eastern Indian music. One night, after an especially meditative music session, I had a dream of a wonderful harp. I was playing this harp that was part sitar and part ancient Egyptian harp. The next day I started building my first harp and when it was finished it sounded as beautiful as its form.

Our music group the A Cid Symphony [in Spanish "To God"], was playing at the Renaissance fair. We were very much absorbed in our music when a three-year-old boy came up and started listening to my harp. He started dancing and his whole body was vibrating to our music. As he reached out to touch the harp, we realized that he was blind. My friends and I were weeping at the enchantment of this magical moment, and later I made another harp and gave it to this young boy. This event touched a special place in me, and I felt the world needed harps. I had found that a harp is tuned to a single scale and when strummed, even by an untrained musician, creates beautifully melodic music. Even without training, it was simple for me to make harmonic background sounds for the music we were playing. I had always wanted to play music although I had never taken the time and the discipline to learn how to play an instrument.

DONOVAN'S SWAN GUITAR, 1971

I made musical instruments, mostly harps, for several years. Very few people seemed to understand the visionary musical instruments I was creating. One musician who did appreciate my work was the popular folk singer, Donovan. He commissioned me to make a guitar that he had seen in one of his dreams. It was in the shape of a swan whose beak held six fish that were the tuning pins. The swans toes were a bridge that held the strings and the sound hole was its heart. When finished,this guitar from the dream world sounded as magical as it looked. Instrument making was a personally fulfilling art form, although after a while I felt I had completed my original creative impulse. By far, the majority of the people who saw my musical creations thought I had gone around the bend. With a somewhat heavy heart, I decided the world was not quite ready for my musical instruments and again I focused my attention on jewelry. The resulting pieces, were separated from my former art work by a quantum leap, as I incorporated my current passions.

While my art work continued to evolve, much of my energy was going into our life style. Plowing our fields with my old hand crank John Deere tractor, building on our house, chopping wood for the long snowy winters and other chores consumed most of my life. Also, I needed to play out many of my childhood fantasies and to celebrate my wildness. Our nearest neighbor, who was an old horse runner, lived on a ranch five miles to the south. Helping him to round up his herd of over a hundred half-mustang horses, was more like play to me than work. To ride over the hill and see his appaloosa stallion turn the herd of mares and drive them away from us at a full run was like riding back into history a hundred years. The horses we were riding were not like the pets I had learned on at my uncle's farm. They had the blood of the original wild horses my neighbor had herded up from Colorado to Washington as a young man.

The horses I had ridden in my youth had never bucked, so I was confused when my chin plowed a foot long furrow on the sod — then I vaguely remembered seeing the horses ears flying under my legs. We laughed about it and eventually I learned to stay on a bucking horse. Later I found out that some of his horses had made it to the Nationals in the rodeo circuit. On a summer day, one of these horses changed the course of my life when she reared up and fell backwards crushing me under her.

I remember the horse rearing up and falling backward, then being in a black void without life. I screamed in rage at my death and my voice echoed all around me. As I continued to scream, the echoing told me that I was in a tunnel sloping upward and I started clawing my way out. There was a speck of light and as I climbed it grew larger until it became the mouth of a cave. I fell out of the cave into my body which was fighting to gasp air into its lungs.

The resulting broken back made it difficult to continue my pioneer, mountain man, wild Indian life style. I found that if I propped up my back by putting the top of a chair under each armpit, I could work at my jewelry bench. Developing an intimate relationship with pain, I continued making jewelry as my body slowly started to mend.

During my time at Merry Field Meadows I had become very impassioned with the ancient art of alchemy. Originally, what attracted me were the rich symbolic drawings that they used to illustrate their manuscripts. Historically, alchemists were portrayed as comical characters who tried to change base metals into gold. According to historical accounts, they did accomplish the transmutation of gold, although it was usually disastrous to them when the local political powers of that time found out. There are stories of alchemists, chained in the towers, making gold for powerful kings, so understandably, they became very secretive about their art. The alchemists developed our present day science of chemistry. As in most ancient traditions, science during the middle ages was honored as a sacred art. The early chemists translated their lab experiments into a mythological allegory that could describe the inner powers of humankind, and how to bring them into harmony.

One aspect of the art of alchemy that touched me deeply was their passion in bringing about a balance of the self. Alchemists traced their teachings to Thoth, the Egyptian god of magic, words and writing, and the consort of the Goddess of truth, Maat. Thoth is the origin of our word truth. The Greeks called Thoth Hermes Tris Magestis [three times great], and to the Romans he was Mercury. In alchemical texts, the gold referred to is often the spiritual gold found by harmonizing the body's energy fields. The alchemists believed that we have wheels of energy in different parts of our body. People the world over have a similar belief, and these centers are usually called by their Sanskrit name chakras [wheels of light]. The intellectual mind chakra seems to overpower the other energy systems and takes us places that are not always best for our whole self. The alchemists worked toward bringing the intellect into balance with the emotional, heart and other chakras.

Their work included the transmutation of the alchemical adept, or magician, out of the world of duality or opposites, into a union and celebration of the perfect balance of life. The alchemists recognized that from the one source of creation, the world of opposites was necessary for the creation of the material world. From the one source came a world of twos: night-day, woman-man, good-bad, sun-moon... Although the appearance of opposites became our lessons in life, we needed to experience again the unity of everything. They called this union the "Philosopher's Stone," and symbolized it as an eagle with two heads. The eagle was the adept in balance, with one head looking at God and the other head looking at Earth.

The alchemical texts also preserved parts of the ancient knowledge of making of amulets and talismans. This ancient art was universally celebrated by our ancestors and resulted in the magical power I could feel radiating from ancient and tribal jewelry pieces. When viewing the ancient jewelry of Egypt and other cultures, I could see that this knowlege was definitely lacking in contemporary jewelry. I wanted to create magical art in this ancient tradition and studied the information available on the subject.

MAGIC

Magic, I learned, is something that we all do at one time or another although for most of us it is unconscious. We use many different words for magic like synchronicity, luck, accident, coincidence and serendipity. The magician learns to use magic in a way that is more controlled and disciplined. The roots of the word "magic" is magh (to make and to be able). The same root word is found in the words "images" and "imagination," both of which are important in the making of magic. Through imagination and images, the magician is able to make things happen in a way that she or he consciously controls. I learned that by using the discipline of magic, my jewelry and sculpture could be made to help heal and protect us as well as teach us about our inner powers.

The alchemical books speak about ceremonies that were used in charging the amulet jewelry piece with a specific power or purpose. These ceremonies sounded very similar to ones used by the Native Americans to "wake up" a medicine object. I started incorporating waking up ceremonies into the process of fabricating the jewelry pieces I created. The new jewelry definitely responded to the ceremonies and something more was happening. I then realized that my new way of celebrating life was affecting my work even more than the ceremonies.

Looking over my shoulder at alchemical books, like they were cookbooks for the making of talismans, would have affected my work very little. Living a life where I was in intimate relationship with the powers that the alchemists had worked with is what transformed my work. The elemental powers of fire, water, earth and air were conjured into my work. The planetary energies in the cosmos around us were called to the pieces influencing them through their astrological positions. Then, the archetypal and animal powers that were needed for a specific purpose were honored for their help in the new art works.

As in ancient times, in order to have the power and life force felt within my art, I needed to have an intimate relationship with all life. I started to see others as mirrors of myself, for we are all part of the same creation and in the same family. All powers, animals, gems, metals and plants are related to the humans and we are all part of the same wheel in the balance of Nature. All aspects of nature are as conscious of our effect on them as we are aware of their effects on us. When meeting with an animal power, I would try to honor them as I would honor a human relation that I love. As a ceremonial artist I would take responsibility for my emotions and how they affect the surrounding trees for they were as sensitive to our innermost feelings as the people with whom we share our lives. Metals and stones were honored for the power, beauty and life that they brought to my art pieces. There could be no interrelationship if stones and metals were viewed as resources, commodities or slave objects without life. To use them otherwise, without reverence, by the supposedly superior "conscious" human beings, would bring imbalance. If honored, all powers would be pleased to be a part of a piece of art that celebrates life and how we all give-away to the circle of balance that is the wheel of creation.

Ancient Egyptian and alchemical symbols often appeared in my new jewelry. My purpose was not to make copies of the art of historical cultures. I was to the best of my ability, using the symbols in the same sacred manner as these ancient artists. When I created a piece using the Egyptian falcon God, Ra, I worked with the power of my personal relationship with falcons. By observing the habits and characteristics of falcons, the Egyptians chose this bird as a mythological symbol of the sun. I aspired to celebrate the ancient deities in a personal way, for I began to understand that ancient symbols may have something to teach us.

The jewelry from this period had an obvious power and depth that my earlier work lacked. One of the people who recognized the new life that my work radiated was Cher. She shared my love for ancient Egyptian culture and commissioned me to do several pieces for her. As more people were attracted to the new pieces in my Los Angeles gallery, I thought it was time to make my work more available by moving back to the center of activity in Southern California. Also, we were facing another long cold winter soon and I was not sure I could chop wood and keep my family warm while my back was healing. After living for seven years in the wilderness, we left Merry Field Meadows and moved south along with the Canadian geese as winter approached from the north.

Winged Sun Circlet / Apis

The Egyptians, as well as many other cultures, recognized that all life is a gift from the sun. They celebrate this gift in their ceremonies, prayers and art. The sun disk, Amon, is often combined with wings and uraeus (snakes). Amon is seen as the creative spirit. The wings show spirit, in animation, coming to Earth. The cobras are the symbol of the Goddess and they were worn on the foreheads of dieties and rulers over the "Third Eye" of insight. The winged sun with serpentine power stood for royal spirit, healing and wisdom.

Apis is the Egyptian name given to the astrological sign of Taurus. He was worshiped as Apis - Osiris, the savior of Egypt. The moon bull was sacrificed in atonement for the sins of the realm. He returned as the Golden Calf in the ceremony of his rebirth. In this aspect. he is associated with Horus, son of Isis.

Cher commissioned me to make this Apis piece, because she was born under the astrological sign of Taurus. Also, like myself, Cher has a strong affinity for the power of Egyptian art.

("Circlet" 24 k gold, silver, "Apis" 24 k gold, jet, ivory, lapis lazuli
turquoise, pipestone, 1974. In the collection of Cher.)

SELENE AND SULIS

The moon, with its cycles of new, increase, full and decrease gave birth to the movement of time, with its cycles of birth, growth, decline and destruction. Because of the connection between womens' "moon" cycles (the nourishment of the womb) and lunar phases, the moon became the prime symbol of the Mother Goddess.

Many ancient cultures saw the Moon Goddess as the Creatress who brooded over the sea until she brought forth Heaven and Earth. The root word for both mind and moon is the Sanskrit "masas" an attribute of the primordial Mother, Ma. The Goddess Europa's name means full moon and the Roman name for the Goddess is Luna. To the Greeks she is Selene the bringer of reason and wisdom.

The moon still indicates the correct time to plant our seeds as my mother taught me. For abundant crops, we plant root crops in the declining moon, and crops above the ground on her increase.

The sun is usually seen as a male deity just as the moon is seen as female. Ancient peoples celebrated the sacred balance of both genders, as the word deity (meaning two) suggests, when they honored the sun.

Our word for sun comes from the Sun Goddess called by the Celtic Britains, Sulis. The Egyptians saw the sun and moon as the eyes of the sky and the Celtic word suil means both eye and sun. Other names for the Sun Goddess that were used by the northern European tribes are Sul, Sol and Sunna.

In Avebury, England, I have sat in ceremony on her pyramid that is now called Silbury Hill. Sulis' 130 foot pyramid overlooks the great stone circle of Avebury and the stone columns that wound like a snake for miles.

("Selene" 24 k gold, silver, electrum, mother-of-pearl,
aquamarine, black onyx, moon stone, crystal, diamond, 1985)

("Sulis" 24 k gold, silver, electrum, amber, topaz,
citrine, rutile quartz, 1985)

("Moon Shield" 24k gold, silver, star sapphire, mother of pearl,
black onyx, moonstone, quartz crystal, 1985)

("Sun Shield" 24k gold, silver, topaz, citrine, fire opal,
quartz crystal, rutile quartz, 1985)

MOON SHIELD / SUN SHIELD

EAGLE MIRROR

The alchemists use the eagle with two heads, looking at both Spirit and Earth, as the archetype of the sacred balance. This piece was my personal shield for several years before I gave it to an Ojibway singer whose grandfather had the medicine of the eagle with two voices. In the Native American world, when the universe has filled us with abundance, a give-away ceremony helps us to complete the circle.

The stones call in the four elemental powers — air, water, earth, and fire. Turquoise reflects the color of the sky and lapis lazuli, the color of the ocean. The green of malachite is the plants, the growing, nurturing power of Earth and ruby her creative fire.

(24k gold silver, yellow star saphire, emerald, ruby, sapphire, lapis lazuli, turquoise, malachite, 1976)

Ra

The call of Ra heralded the news of creation. He was the father of the gods and man, and while he ruled a golden age existed in which gods and man could live together happily.

With its soaring flight, the falcon was a natural choice for the Egyptians as the representative of the god of the sky. Each morning Ra, as the sun, rose in the east and set off across the Heavens in his solar barge to set in the west at night.

(Silver, enamel, lapis lazuli, turquoise, carnelian, 1976)

UNICORN SONG

Two Celtic harps sing the story of unicorns dancing in the forest. From the unicorn's forehead, a single golden, spiral horn projects. This is at the point of the Third Eye, the place of the spiritual cognition center of the brain. The spiral horn reflects the movements of creative energy observed everywhere in Nature from the spiral of our DNA molecules to the vast vortex of our galaxy.

The alchemists adapted the unicorn as the symbol of the illumined spiritual nature of an initiate. Like the human quest after spirit, the unicorn is magical and elusive.

Allegorically, the bards sing of a way to capture the unicorn through the help of a maiden who sits alone in the woods. Her purity is said to attract the unicorn, who approaches the maid and lays its head in her lap. If we enter into one of our Earth Mother's pristine forests, with a childlike innocence, we may encounter there our spiritual essence.

(24 k gold, silver, electrum, sugilite, amethyst, 1987)

POINT DUME
LIFE IN THE FAST LANE

Knowing that it would be difficult to integrate our life back into Los Angeles after living in the wilderness, we settled in Point Dume, Malibu. Malibu escapes much of the intensity of being in L A because it is protected by the Santa Monica Mountains on one side and the Pacific Ocean on the other. When the pressures of city life became too great I could escape into the mountain canyons in back of my house or the beach in front.

Many of our neighbors were celebrities from the nearby movie, music, and television industries. Several of these people were attracted to my art work and some of them became personal friends. Either consciously or unconsciously, I think the Hollywood personalities were responding to the protective quality of the pieces. In our archetypally starved culture we often give our celebrities the power that was at one time given to our heros, goddesses, and gods. Historically, our archetypal myths represented our different energy centers and the stories were meant to give clues on how to bring them and ourselves into balance. The lack of a traditional myth to help us understand our life creates a void within us that we try to fill with our adoration of famous people.

This energy that is sent toward the celebrities is often erratic and destructive and my jewelry pieces were able to assist with their individual protective powers. We all have the ability to protect ourselves and keep the unbalanced energy away that people send toward us. The magical jewelry piece is merely a focus and celebration of our own power. To place too much dependence on a person or object would be to give away our own personal power.

I feel that because my intent was to charge the jewelry with protection, it was helping the celebrities to deal with this misplaced energy. Many of these people let me know that the jewelry was helping them and that it "felt" good or protected when wearing a piece. Some of the personalities that I made pieces for during this time were: Joan Baez, Carol Burnett, Glenn Campbell, Cher, Neil Diamond, Bob Dylan, Michael Jackson, Elton John, Stevie Nicks, George Harrison, Jonie Mitchell and Cheryl Tiegs. It was fulfilling to have my work touch people who had a world wide influence.

The magic in my work was gaining momentum and taking my career to new heights. Artistic excellence and beauty had always been the primary concern in my work, although I also dreamed about being rich and famous. In my early art pieces, career success was certainly a strong motivation. With my later art work, the energy of a piece became much more important. My vision of creating magical art started to manifest and brought with it, unexpectedly, the career success I had fantasized about as a young man.

Many people laugh at magic until they need it and then they will pray or get a horoscope drawn. To embrace the belief that we can magically affect our environment, we also have to embrace the fact that we are responsible for our environment. It seems that most people refuse magic because they do not to want to accept the responsibility that we can control our environment instead of it controlling us.

When life offers me a new experience, I like to jump in with both feet — not test the water with my toe. We went from living in a hand built cabin to a four bedroom beach house and from driving an old pickup truck to a shining Bentley. Transplanting part of our former lifestyle to our new home, ours was the only Malibu house with a tipi in the back yard and a Gypsy wagon in the driveway.

Films started using my pieces in them and it was amazing to see my work magnified on the silver screen. Even the film industry seemed to recognize the magical quality of the jewelry. The film, "King of the Gypsies," commissioned me to do the talisman medallion that was worn by the Gypsy king. Sometimes my work found its way into songs of friends that were songwriters. Jonie Mitchell mentioned my jewelry in a song and Bob Dylan sang about Sara's Isis necklace in his song "Isis" on the Desire album.

The demands that this new lifestyle made on my family and I were physically, mentally, and emotionally stressful. I was filled with so many ideas and visions that wanted to be created that I was often overwhelmed. The creative Muses seemed to be dancing with me continually, even at night as I tried to sleep. It was not uncommon for me to work 18 hour days and sometimes I would work around the clock without sleep. There was definitely an imbalance in my workaholism that was very self-destructive. Without the lessons that I had learned in my time in the wilderness, I'm not sure that I would have survived L A and life in the fast lane.

When the passionate creative fire seemed to be consuming me, I would walk on the beach or in the mountains. Finding a private, secluded spot, I would meditate or sit in ceremony with my sacred pipe. Sometimes I would fast for a few days and sit in vision quest on Boney Mountain, the highest peak in the Santa Monicas. During these times, Nature would nurture, heal and help me regain my balance. Within 40 miles of L A, sometimes I could walk all day in the Santa Monica mountains without seeing another person. During my time in the wilderness I would encounter many animal powers including eagles, deer, rattlesnakes and even mountain lions.

The time spent in the mountains helped me to balance the demands of my L A life style. With the pressures of movie deals; commissions from super stars; family; friends; lovers; and financial obligations, there was never a tranquil moment in my mind. Visionquest gave me a time when I could sit with a quiet mind and be the silent observer. Apart from my outer life, I could experience my inner life. What I found, sitting alone for days on a mountain, was a better understanding of who I was and the unlimited power that is locked within my soul. Also I experienced boredom, cold, loneliness, frustration and fear.

One time, I bushwhacked my way up a side canyon to find a remote spot to meditate for a few days. The biting cold of winter pressed in on me that night under the clear moonless sky that was filled with stars. As I sat in wonder of the surrounding beauty, a mountain lion screamed a dozen feet behind me. It was not the first time that I had heard this sound. There were cougars around our place in Washington and the sound they make resembles a woman screaming. It made the hair stand up on my neck. The sound is an efficient way to make its prey stand frozen while the big lion pounces. My rational mind knew that mountain lions do not attack humans, however, I did not feel rational and I thought I was drawing my last breath. I did not die under claws and fangs of the lion although the screams continued throughout that sleepless night.

As twilight arrived and I could finally see, I turned and there behind me was a huge owl. It flew off into the morning and the sunrise was like a rebirth for me. In our ancestral tribes, an elder would help to integrate the experiences we encountered on vision quest. Without this help, I honored the opportunity to experience fear, death and rebirth and the new day that was filled with life.

THE SWEAT LODGE
About this time, I was introduced to the Native American sweat lodge ceremony. This ancient ceremony varies with different tribes although it usually includes the same elements. A small lodge is made by sticking saplings in the ground forming a circle and binding them into an arc about chest high. Blankets are placed over the sticks so that it is completely dark inside. Rocks are heated to red hot in a fire and then placed into a hole in the earth inside the lodge. All aspects in the preparing of the lodge are treated with reverence to the elements that are helping to form this circle of power.

The sweat lodge chief and the people say "all my relations" upon entering the lodge as a prayer to everyone in the universe. As we sit in the darkness, water is poured over the hot rocks that hiss with steam. In this sacred space, we take turns singing songs and offering our prayers for healing and balance. The lodge is like the dark womb of our Mother Earth and when we crawl out of the lodge into the light, we are cleaned like a newborn baby.

In the past when I had walked into a church, cathedral or ancient temple, I was somehow cast out of myself into a spiritually receptive place. Inside this humble little earth lodge, I found an even greater connection with spirit. The ceremonies touched me so deeply, I decided that I would build a lodge in our back yard. I knew where saplings grew on a friend's property and resolved to gather some on my next visit. However, by the time that I got around to going there I had forgotten my plan.

After hiking around, I was sitting in ceremony by the stream and a small falcon lit in the tree close above me. She started to sing and kept the song going during the ceremony. I noted the direction that she flew away in and decided to follow her. When I arrived in the area she had flown to, she had left me a gift, one of her flight feathers. As I was offering her tobacco, I realized that I was standing in the middle of the saplings. I definately knew that it was time to cut the long sticks and to build my sweat lodge. Two decades later, the little feather is still helping us in my medicine bundle when we do a sweat lodge ceremony.

Another ceremony that I was working with in Malibu was the sacred pipe ceremony. For years I had used the "peace" pipe in my personal prayers, and as I started to lead sweat lodge ceremonies the pipe took on a deeper meaning for me. I realized that within the responsibility of running a sweat lodge for my friends, I was beginning to put on the robe of a medicine person. A Paiute sweat lodge chief gifted me with a piece of pipestone to carve into a new ceremonial pipe. When it was finished, my first ceremony was to wake up the pipe, sitting on Point Dume overlooking the ocean.

SANTA BARBARA 1979

Point Dume is the point of land that is seen jutting out on the map above the sweeping arc of L A harbor. Sitting on the tip, there is a 270 degree view of the ocean and I could feel the power of thousands of years of ceremonies that our ancestors had performed there. As I called the powers to the pipe, a lizard watched me and crows flew over my head.

In placing the tobacco into the pipe, I called in all the powers of the universe. With the first pinch of tobacco I called the Mother Earth and then Father Sky, followed by the powers that come to us from the four cardinal directions of the compass. Next I honored the center on the wheel, the protective powers that surround the wheel, the powers of nature with all trees and other growing people, all the animal powers, and the sacred grandparents of the spirit world. I offered the pipe to all the assembled powers before I smoked the pipe myself. With the smoke, I sent the voice of my prayers to all the corners of the universe. As I smoked, looking out over the ocean, a fish hawk swooped over my head and out to the water after a fish. I followed its flight until it was out of the range of my vision. At the moment it disappeared I saw the spouting of the family of whales that had also come to our ceremony.

There is a story I would like to tell to show how precious this medicine pipe is to me. During a Santa Ana wind storm blowing 90 degree winds of 60 miles per hour down the mountains toward the sea, there was a huge brush fire. These brush fires in Southern California play a natural part in the life and death cycles of the native vegetation. What causes them to be disasters is that we build our houses in their path. The fire started 20 miles inland and we thought that it would be put out long before it threatened our home. Within a short time it had roared over the ridge in back of our house.

My neighbors told me that the brush fires move so fast that if I was on the roof to swat out sparks with a wet towel, the fire would pass by my house. Standing on top of my house as a hundred foot wall of flames raced down the hills, I was starting to wonder about the wisdom of being on the roof with a wet towel in my hand. The wind in front of the fire was ferocious and I was mesmerized by the whirlwinds that sent columns of fire hundreds of feet in the air. They looked like huge fire elementals dancing with wild abandon. When the wind roared in my direction, I could see nothing except blinding smoke and flashing sparks. There were burning limbs the size of my arm whirling through the wind that picked up my tipi to deposit it a hundred yards away. Then as the wind shifted, I could see several houses burning in the surrounding hills out of the 200 homes that perished in the Malibu blaze. The few neighbors and myself who stayed behind on our roofs, saved all the houses on our block.

This adventure is a memorial experience, however the part that stands out in my memory is what happened before I climbed onto the roof. The people in our neighborhood were riding their horses to the beach or loading up their cars for a fast getaway. The speed of the approcing flames left just enough time to evacuate our children, pets and a few belongings down to the beach. After we put our children in the car, Joan and I returned to rescue as many things as we could. I first ran into my studio where my gemstones, gold, tools, jewelry... were kept and then grabbed my pipe from my altar. In that split second, I realized I was holding my most treasured object in my hands.

To celebrate putting on a the robe of a medicine person and the trans- formative powers that were changing me, I decided it was time to change my name. In the Native American tradition and in many other cultures throughout the world, people change their name at some point in their life. The name change may come after an initiation ceremony, after a vision quest with auspicious signs or at the time of a life passage. At birth I was named Edward, and at different times I was also called Eddie or Ed. The person that was chosen to conduct a sweat lodge or wedding ceremony was starting not to feel like Ed.

There were many medicine animals that had come to me during vision quest and in my dreams. The jaguar, owl, eagle, deer, rattlesnake, coyote and others could have become my medicine name. Also, the tradition of the heyoka or contrary seemed to be very much a part of who I was.

For thousands of years, many Native American peoples governed them- selves by a democracy based on the council circle. No law could pass the cir- cle unless it was debated and unanimously accepted by all the women and men who sat in the circle. The persons who formally introduced any new law into the circle were the heyokas. They were often the more creative peo- ple in the tribes and were likely to be the artists. They helped the council to look at all the effects that the new law would have. They did this by act- ing out the law in hilarious ways — dressing up in it, turning it upside down and inside out. They were the sacred clowns.

Artists are the heyokas of today in American society. With our govern- ment and our institutions becoming more and more deaf to the needs of the people, it is usually the artists, writers, song-lyricists, and film stars who hurl the call for a new law into the circle. Or they dress up in the old law and clown around to show us how bad it is. Also, the modern heyokas bring into the circle new visions of the ancient myths that were once an important part of our culture.

All of this information was put into my sacred pipe as I meditated on the choice of a new name. I had read that in certain tribes, a person knew they were a heyoka person when they dreamed of lightning, and I could not remember having such a dream. I knew it was time for a new name and I waited for an auspicious sign.

In my dream I was growing long eagle wings. As sometimes happens for me, my conscious mind was awake while I slept. I was very elated because flying dreams are my favorite kind. After a flying dream I wake up feeling exhilarated and energized. I soared through the sky and then I saw a huge thunder cloud. I flew into the middle of the cloud and then remembered that a heyoka dreams of lightning. Lightning shot out of my body in all directions and when I awoke I knew that I had been given my new name, "Heyoka."

MEDICINE
TEACHERS

During this time of my life, I wanted very much to have a wise teacher to teach me the medicine path. My wish connected me with several teachers. Some of these teachers helped me to learn how to walk in a balanced way on our life's journey. Other teachers "talked" a lot about how to live in a sacred way although when I looked at their actions and life, their main teaching was how not to live my life.

Grandmother Evelyn Eaton adopted me as her grandson during one of my ceremonies. This wise old medicine woman taught me much about ceremony and how to become an elder with dignity and honor. On a trip to Montana, I met my Crow sundance chief. He was another grandparent who taught me much by the power and integrity of his life.

There were also medicine teachers who could talk the talk but not live the life of a medicine person. I found these unbalanced teachers eloquent speakers, but their lives were about lies; conning people out of their money and personal power; controlling the less charismatic people near them; and sexual abuse. After several painful encounters, I returned to honoring Nature as my primary teacher. I also found there is much to learn from ourselves, following the impulses that originate in our heart. If my own impulses were improper, it would soon be reflected back to me as an imbalance in my life or surrounding environment.

When we moved back to L A, we had made a pledge to ourselves that we would stay for only five years, then move back to a rural area. Too many times I had known people who would move to L A for a little while to complete a project and then buy a piece of land in the country. Often these people would spend the rest of their lives living in L A waiting for their dream to happen. After our five years were finished, we had experienced tremendous financial success and also we had spent every bit of it on our Hollywood lifestyle. When we finally moved out of town, the only money we took with us was from selling our Bentley motorcar. We had no clue where we were moving to, except away from L A. We put our furniture in storage, loaded our tipi on top of the van, and drove out of town.

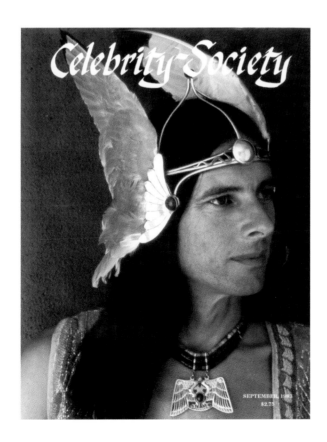

LOS ANGELES 1983

THE KING'S MEDALLION

For the film "King of the Gypsies," the symbol of a cross within the circle was chosen. The story was about the talisman passing through three generations of gypsy kings. The circle is a female symbol sacred to the Great Goddess showing the cyclic motion of life. The cross is a male symbol and represents the powers that come to us from the four directions called by many different names including the Sacred Grandparents, the Four Pillars and the Archangels.

The origin of the gypsy tribes was Hindustan where these two symbols shown together are a sign of sexual union. Gypsies would use the magic of these two emblems to keep their horses from running away. By marking one on each front leg of a horse, the two drawings would attract one another and draw the horse's feet together like a hobble.

(24 k gold, silver, brass, lapis lazuli, 1978.
Designed for the film "King of the Gypsies,"
starring Sterling Hayden, Shelley Winters,
Susan Sarandon, Brook Shields and Eric Roberts.)

FLYING MOUSE

When a friend first asked me to do a bat necklace for a Dracula film I was very hesitant. I could not with good conscience diabolize an animal power in my work. However, after reading the script I realized that the movie was a delightful comedy.

The bat means good fortune and great happiness in the Orient. In ancient Europe, our pagan ancestors associated the bat with the flight of our soul during sleep or after death. Later these ancestral spirits became the bat "demons" that are so popular in Hollywood.

One of the Medicine powers of the bat to the Native Americans is guardian of the night. This association does not mean that the bat (Flying Mouse) is an evil power, because night is not seen as fearful or evil. Night is the reflection of day, the one cannot exist without the other. The bat is a helper through our darkest hour.

Flying Mice do another service for humankind that I celebrate. Each night they can eat their weight in a somewhat troublesome animal power — mosquitos.

(24 k gold, silver, garnets, crystal, 1979.
Designed for the film "Love at First Bite," starring
Susan Saint James and George Hamilton.)

One of the great joys of my career has been making pieces for various celebrities. The most meaningful of these relationships has surrounded ceremonial objects that I have created for George Harrison over the last two decades. On many levels I feel a deep kinship with him especially in his personal commitment to his spiritual evolution.

George has been supportive and appreciative of the discipline that I have chosen to be my life's work. His commissions have often pushed me to new levels of achievement and his selection of my works include some of my all time favorites.

Pictured here are a few of the pieces that are in his collection. Clockwise from the top: jamming in the studio; his personal shield (the first piece I made for him); Olivia Harrison with Unicorn Necklace and Priestess crown; George and Olivia's rings; Yogananda shrine (open and folded); and in the center, my favorite, is his traveling Ganesha shrine.

FLASH GORDON

During my time in Malibu, it seemed like there was always a movie that was interested in my work. Most of these films never were made and some of them were made without using my pieces. The pieces pictured here were for the film Flash Gordon.

("Winged Crown" silver, 24k, emerald; "Ra" silver, lapis lazuli, carnelian; "Isis and Ra belt" silver, lapis lazuli, carnelian, 1979)

SEA GULL SHIELD / SWAN MIRRORS / LOTUS BELT

Sea gulls are the keepers of sea shores. This is the place where the physical body—earth meets the emotional body—ocean. One day as I was walking on the beach I found a dead sea gull lying in the sand. As I marveled at the beauty of the wings, I knew that this keeper of the shores wanted to live on in a medicine shield.

The piece that resulted from this encounter, was a winged crown. Diadems, crowns or hats are often viewed as insignias of office or status. I see head shields as protectors of the "crown" chakra, the energy center that connects us with our higher self.

It is reasonable to see why swans were chosen to be the keeper of the dreamtime. When we see a swan gliding upon the mirror of a still pond, we are easily carried into a quiet, dreamy receptivity. In the Vedic mythology, the godhead Brahma, rides upon the back of a swan. In the Greek myth, Zeus in a swan form impregnated Leda. From this union, Leda gave birth to twilight, dawn and the moon. Swans also symbolized the Muses that brought, through artists, inspirations from the dream world.

The lotus flower is symbolic of the Great Goddess. In India she is called the golden lotus, Mytripadma, womb of life. The Egyptians saw her as Hathor, the lotus from whom the sun was born at his first rising. Within the cosmic womb the four elements of creation were united. The element of earth is the mud in which the lotus is rooted, while the stalk is supported by the surrounding water. The blossom opens above the surface releasing its perfume into the air where the fire of the sun impregnates the flower with fertility. When the Buddha could not find words to tell his students what had happened to him as he sat beneath the tree of enlightenment, he held up a lotus flower.

("Sea Gull Shield" 24 k gold, silver, copper, lapis lazuli, sea gull wings, 1974)

("Swan Mirrors" 24 k gold, silver, black opal, lapis lazuli, 1975.
In the collection of Stevie Nicks.)

("Lotus Belt" 24 k gold, silver, black opal, 1976. A flower belt is in
the collection of Cheryl Tiegs.)

OUR LADY OF THE LAKE
IN THE WIND

We left the City of Angels in the spring, planning to live in our van and tipi while we traveled around the Western States. We were visiting all the places we loved, Santa Fe, Aspen, Sun Valley and many areas we had only heard about. As we visited each part of the country we were open for a spot to speak to us, wanting us to live there. The only schedule we were committed to was being on the Crow reservation in midsummer where I planned to sundance. One of my sweat lodge chiefs had advised me not to worry about where we were moving, "just to focus on the Sundance and after the dance everything will be clear."

BEVERLY HILLS SHOW 1983

It was a delightful time wandering around the country and if a place felt good we would put up the tipi for a week or two so we could feel the rhythms of the land. While we were in Taos, we stayed with an old grandfather. We were talking about the Sundance as he gave me an offering of tobacco to take to the dance. He told me to go into the sundance lodge completely empty and allow the dance to fill me.

As midsummer approached, we drove to the ancestral land of the Crow People. The Sundance lasts three or four days and there are many rites in the weeks before the dance preparing for the ceremony. We set up the tipi near the house of our sundance chief so we could help with the activities leading up to the dance.

Each step in the preparation of the lodge is treated with reverence and respect. Before a tree was cut down for the ceremony, we smoked a pipe and offered prayers to the tree in appreciation for its sacrifice to the lodge. On the morning of the dance, a large round lodge was built, open to the sky above. In the center of the lodge was the sundance tree.

At sunrise, standing where the sundance tree would be put, we had burned cedar and honored the sun with our prayers. The place the sun rose was noted because the door of the lodge is placed in the east where the sunrise will shine in. As we turned our backs to the glowing sunrise, the western sky was as black as night from a huge storm. In front of the darkness was the blazing arc of a rainbow. In the middle of the arc was our tipi, and it was the only tipi out of the scores of tents in the Indian encampment. It was about noon and Grandmother Eaton was braiding my hair for the dance when the storm hit.

The Crow Indians had joked about the breed boy from California having the only tipi in camp. It was a zealously lusty Montana thunder storm. When it left the ceremony, the people were marveling about the wisdom of their ancient designs when our brightly painted tipi was one of the few tents that was not destroyed by the wind's ferocity.

The day before, we had left the plains and gone into the mountains to gather the small fur trees that surrounded the lodge. It was a day of ceremony and very hard work with the cutting down and hauling of the trees. I lost my wallet on the mountain. I felt dazed, being with my family in the middle of the prairie without my cash, credit cards, drivers licence, or identification. Then, I remembered my grandfather's words in Taos, "be completely empty when you enter the sundance lodge."

To the steady heartbeat of the drum, we started our dancing in the evening. After weeks of activity, I found myself surrendering completely to the ceremony as I danced to the sundance tree. I began to understand that when we work with Mother Nature in the Sundance, we need to respect the way a tree experiences life. While we breathe in oxygen and exhale carbon dioxide, the sundance tree breathes in carbon dioxide and exhales oxygen. We are symbiotic and depend upon each other for our life giving breath. A tree breathes once a day and we breathe thousands of times a day. The much slower trees usually perceive us as a blur of moving energy much like we would experience a lightning being. In the Sundance, while fasting food and water, we danced in the same place during the three day ceremony. As we danced back and forth, we made paths on the ground that looked like the spokes of a wheel radiating out from the tree. They reminded me of the many different paths that the universe bestowed on us that will lead us back to the center. While we danced in the same spot, the tree was able to have an intimate relationship with us for the space of three of her breaths.

Our sundance tree was a forked tree to show that when we leave the universe of the one power, the world becomes split into opposites. The two forks split into limbs that were the many families of life, animals, people, fish, rocks, plants, birds... The leaves were the many types in each family as in all the races of people. On the branches of the cottonwood tree, all the wind-blown leaves reflected the life-giving sunlight to each other like shimmering mirrors. In the underworld were the roots which reminded me of the ancient teaching, "that which is below is as that which is above." The visible world reflects the invisible world. Like the universe, all parts of the sundance tree are one, and each segment is necessary for the life of the tree.

On the third day of the ceremony, the people who were ill removed their shoes and came into the lodge. While standing next to the tree, our sundance chief prayed for healing and doctored them with his eagle fan and otter skin. The sundance tree helped our chief by using her power to give healing to the people from the Earth. The women and men sundancers added their energy to the healing by dancing to the tree. As we danced, blowing our eagle bone whistles, it sometimes felt like we were dancing in and out of the world.

Continuing our journey after the dance I often felt that a part of me was still in another world. We camped in Yellowstone for a couple of weeks while I tried to integrate what had happened to me at the dance. After Yellowstone we made our way through Idaho, always looking for our spot. Since we were close to where we had lived in Washington, we decided to visit our old neighbors whom we had not seen for several years. When our neighbors found out we were looking for land they started suggesting places they knew of.

Having lived in this area before, I wanted to experience living somewhere else. What we found is that land costs so much more in places like Santa Fe that we could not afford to live there. I had this vision of what I wanted the property to be like. A forested area with expansive views and a cascading stream running through the land down to a river. We found the place in my dreams near where we had lived before in Merry Field Meadows.

The preparing of our land for the roads and buildings became a ceremony. We offered our prayers to the spirits of the land explaining how and why we were cutting into the Earth. We would ask permission of the trees that gave their life in order to make space for the buildings. As we marked the trees that had to be removed we would thank them for the gift of life they were giving to our dream for a home. We explained that we would be good stewards and neighbors with treekind and the trees that died would be made into boards and continue to live on in the buildings.

When I started cutting down the trees, it was so traumatic that I decided to cut just the ones on the building sights. The marked trees that would have let more sunlight into the buildings were not cut down. The following year, the marked trees that were left standing were blown over by a great wind that came through the land. It felt like the trees were able to understand our needs and accepted our living on the land with their give-away.

For years I had made my art in garages, basements or bedrooms and my dream was to have a studio in which to do my work and ceremony. In building my earth sheltered studio, I tried to make it blend and balance with the natural environment, by using earth as a natural insulation; it is cool in the summer and retains the warmth of the wood stove in the winter. All the windows are in the south of the building so the winter sun, low on the southern horizon will shine into the windows and help heat the room. In the long days of the northern summer, the windows are always in the shade so there is no heat gain. One of my favorite architects is the Spanish artist Gaudi and he influenced the design of my studio. It is like a smooth round organic cave inside. It reminds me of the womb of the Earth Mother where the creation of my art may materialize. From the sanctuary of my studio my imagination, visions and dreams can be born.

SEPARATION

While the studio was under construction, my marriage came to an end. When Joan and our children moved back to California, I realized that my family had been for me some of my greatest of joys. In being separated from my family, I experienced some of the greatest depressions of my life.

After our divorce, it felt like there was a sort of a completion in my relationship with Joan and that perhaps our karmic time of learning together had come to an end. It never occurred to me that our friendship would also end or that my children would break off all contact with me. In California, my family joined a sect that manipulates its members into having very little contact with family members or friends outside what they call the Army. My family met the leader of this group when I worked with him for a while until his teachings started to feel to me unbalanced and fanatical. He started by teaching Native American wisdom, although he eventually changed the teachings into a para-military hierarchy in which he became the general.

Joan and the girls continued to make the ceremonial art that was so much a part of our life together. Years later, a friend showed me a necklace that she said reminded her of my work. Tears came to my eyes as I saw that the beautiful and powerful piece was created by one of my daughters, realizing that a part of me is still with them. Fundamentalism may be a quick cure for personal problems, however, I see it as causing many of our planetary problems. To me, when fundamentalist groups, whether they are Christian, Moslem, Native American or any other say that everyone outside their sect is lost, a sinner, damned, or the enemy, then they are condemning part of themselves.

As my daughters were born into my hands and they took their first breath, I experienced an epiphany that is still unsurpassed in my life. In our time together, Joan was very supportive to me as we moved around the country chasing our dreams. Since I worked at home, I was able to spend a lot of quality time with Isis, Ishtar and Astarte. Our family was so close and bonded that it was hard for me to find my identity separate from them. It was winter when I moved out of our home and into the half completed studio. I found myself once more living by myself in the wilderness.

Camping out in the cold unfinished studio, I spiraled down into the darkness of my soul. From the ecstasy of family to the agony of separation came a deep emptiness. This was a time of mourning that resulted in a feeling of apathy but I worked to transmute the energy of my depression into new creations of art. I was not alone, for outside there were my family of the trees and animals. There were my friends the creek, the sun, the moon and all of Nature. The Muses kept me company helping to inspire me with new artistic visions. My work helped to heal me and helped me to remember my passion for life.

For the first seven years I lived without electricity, hauling my water from the creek. I worked on my art and in my spare time continued building on the studio. Living without the modern conveniences was not a problem except for not having a shower. At times like this, necessity can be the mother of invention — or in the local jargon, we can make a "farmer rig." This problem was solved by building a fire under a 30 gallon water tank outside with a shower head attached to it. A gasoline driven water pump was put by the creek and when started it provided water pressure for the tank. Pulling the rope to start the motor also started the shower so I had to run, sometimes through the snow, to the shower. At this point, even when standing in the snow, I had a wonderfully hot, steamy, shower for about 10 minutes. The only problem was that the hot shower ended abruptly, when the ice cold creek water suddenly came out of the shower head.

During this time, I felt the need to hunt for a deer for my winter's meat. At one point in my life I had become a vegetarian for over a decade. I became sensitive to the feeling of the death in my meat so I stopped eating animals. Eventually I became as sensitive to the world of plants as I was to animals. Because I needed to eat in order to live it was necessary for me to understand that we are all part of the wheel of death and life. When we die, our body returns to the earth and feeds both the plants and animals. What was missing for me was the reverence and honoring for the beings that die so that we may live. Animals and plants understand how we all give away to the circle of life and death. They give their life to us open-heart-edly if we take the time to celebrate their gift with reverence and ceremony. Now that I was again eating meat, I needed to complete the circle in the ceremony of killing a deer.

In a sweat lodge, I purified myself to get ready for the hunt. I prayed to the deer that was to give-away to me and explained that I needed the energy that the meat could bequeath to me that winter. After smudging with sweetgrass, I went hunting by the first light of morning. After walking a short distance, a deer walked in front of me. Lifting my rifle and taking aim I could not pull the trigger because my heart was pounding so hard that it was shaking my barrel. Tobacco was offered to this deer and then I continued hunting. Four days later on my way up a ridge, a deer jumped out of a bush and ran to the left. I thought I should follow the deer but my intuitions told me to continue up the ridge. As I walked over the ridge, the deer had doubled back and was in front of me breathing hard.

I felt the calmness of the give-away as I raised my rifle and fired. There was direct eye contact as the second shot took the deer's life. Pointing the head toward the east, tobacco was sprinkled around the deer as I sang my medicine song in honoring. I said that I would use in a good and honorable way the life force that was gifted to me. As the deer became a part of my body so will I give away of my body to the earth when I die. At that time I will become food for the grass who will feed future generations of deer. As the deer became part of me, I will become part of the deer within the circle of life. To this day, the intensity of the deer's death in this hunting ceremony helps me to pause before I eat. I thank the plants or animals and I honor the gift of their life in my food.

Living alone on the land, I started to reconnect with the rhythms of the Earth. The hardships and joys of living close to Nature was healing the scars left in my being from the loss of my family and from the hyper-active life style of L A. From all the responsibilities, obligations and distractions of contemporary life, I hardly knew who I was. Pushing myself way beyond the limits of my physical powers had left me exhausted to the very marrow of my bones. I knew when I was living in Los Angeles, that I was pushing myself to a degree that was unhealthy. I thought that as soon as I stopped overworking I would be normal again . What I found that was the habits that had become a part of my life were taking years to once again come into a balance.

My vision for the property was not to create a safe refuge where I could escape from the outside world. I wanted the land to become a spiritual retreat and a center of learning for magical and ceremonial art. My dream was not to be the owner of the land, simply the caretaker, priest and teacher responsible for helping young people to awaken their artistic and spiritual potential. While still in L A, I had started to manifest this dream when I formed a non-profit educational, religious and charitable foundation.

One of our greatest American architects, Frank Lloyd Wright, formed a similar foundation with his Taliesin East and West. This foundation, even after the death of this renowned artist, still continues to teach young artists. The teaching approach is in the old traditional format of a master/apprentice relationship. Rather than classroom focused learning, experienced artists teach a few apprentices at a time by doing the art work together. In the beginning his students learned architecture by helping to design and build their own school and living quarters. Now they learn by working closely with other master architects on actual buildings. Many arts, including music, theater and dance are part of the students' activities. At Taliesin, Wright's philosophy of how to make architecture blend and integrate with the Earth is a meaningful part of the learning process. Wright said of Taliesin, in the foundation's catalogue: "I want these young people to learn to drink from the source, whether I am here or not. They will develop their own technique."

At times there has been an amazing support for my vision of a center for ceremony and art. People have donated their time, ideas and resources to the building and development of my dream. Friends and apprentices have labored on our studios and offered their prayers for the land. I have received remarkable support from my partner Katherine, when the enormity of this lifelong project becomes too overwhelming. The world wide acceptance of my art work is satisfying, however my apprentices have brought an even greater sense of accomplishment to my life. One of my European apprentices who seemed like a wounded soul when we met wrote me later, ..."Spring greetings from DK! You know, making jewelry is probably the best thing that has happened in my life." The world seems to have lost something important when we went from the apprentice system to the classrooms. The intimate master/apprentice relationship gives me the opportunity to give back to the future generations that which the universe has gifted to me.

The foundation's property is bordered by the Columbia River, which has been expanded into an immense lake from the Grand Coulee dam. Because of its size, this hundred and fifty mile long lake feels more like an inland sea. Sometimes as we ride the ferry across this body of water to our land, it seems like we are returning through the mists to the magical Island of Avalon. The official name of the lake is Franklin D. Roosevelt, which to me never seemed to honor the power and beauty of this young lake. The energy of the lake feels feminine and my personal name for the lake is Lady of the Lake. This was the title of the high priestess of Avalon who gave the sword of kingship, Excaliber to Arthur in the old stories. In meditating upon a name for the land, I realized that the most omnipotent elemental power here was the lake. In honor of the energy of this great water spirit we named the land Our Lady of the Lake.

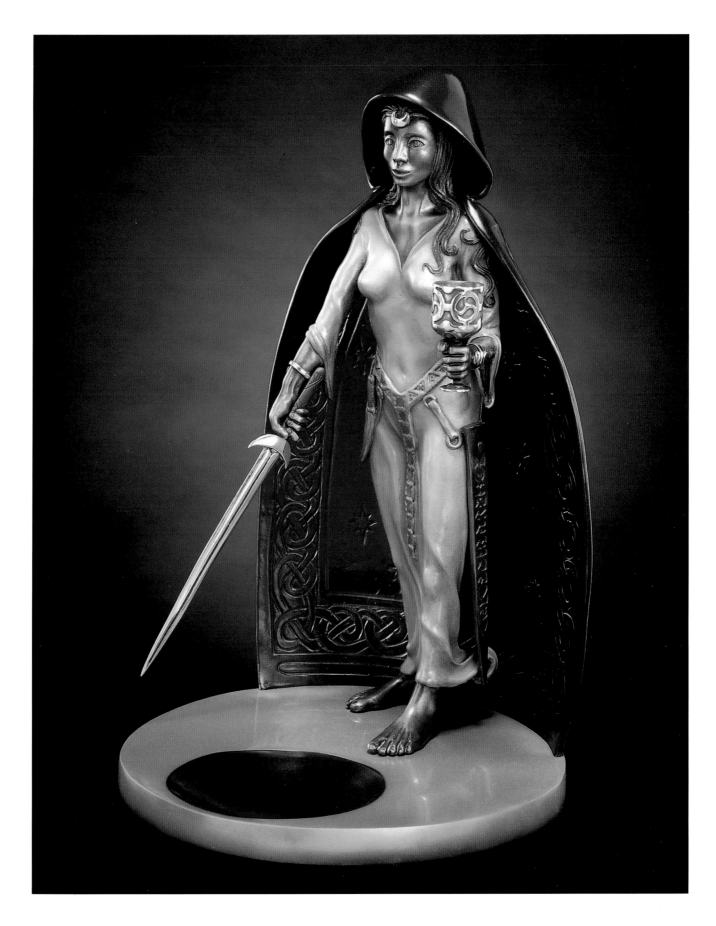

LADY OF THE LAKE

(Bronze, 13 inches, limited edition of 30)

LADY OF THE LAKE

Lady of the Lake, Viviane, Morgane, Ceridwen, Nimaway, Brigid and many other names are all aspects of the great mother Goddess of the Celtic people. We are familiar with many of these goddesses as the women in the tales of King Arthur and the knights of the Round Table. This story resonates strongly in us because it speaks in the language of the archetypal powers that are a part of our western culture.

Viviane (she who lives), the Lady of the Lake, high priestess of Britain was the earthly manifestation of the Goddess. Sovereignty and kingship could be bestowed only by the the high priestess. The women of Avalon forged the magic sword Excaliber and gave this sword of kingship to Arthur. Excaliber is also the sword of truth, which can sever the world of illusion from the world of reality.

She lived at Glastonbury Tor, which was called the island of Avalon before the surrounding lake was drained to destroy her power. On the Isle of the Apples or Avalon, the bees would take the magical richness of her apples back to the four quarters of the ordinary world. She had the power to bestow sovereignty, wisdom, inspiration, and skill in craft.

Lady of the Lake was keeper of the sacred cauldron of rebirth and transformation. Her chalice or cauldron was an inexhaustible divine food source for the soul. She was a healer and a drink from one of her sacred wells often brought healing. When Arthur was wounded, the Lady of the Lake took him to the sacred Isle to be healed. Sometimes a drink from her cauldron or her well would turn an ordinary man into a bard or even a king.

With the death of King Arthur, Lancelot returns the sword Excaliber to the lake. In this way the sovereignty of kingship was returned to the Lady of the Lake and into the keeping of the Goddess.

(Bronze, 13 inches, limited edition of 30, 1990)

on page 67

The Wind Sang to Me

At sunset, I was playing the harp out on my studio's deck which overlooks the Columbia River. It was a warm summer evening and the breeze was starting to stir as the sun was setting. This was one of the times that I found myself living alone in the Northwest wilderness, and I was celebrating this time of solitude with Nature — also I was feeling a bit lonely.

The wind started to vibrate the strings of my harp and, as I put my ear to the sound-box to hear the delicate sounds, incredible music flowed from the wind thru my harp. The presence of the wind was very tactile and it felt as though she was caressing me in an embrace as she flowed around me and played my harp. It was a nurturing touch that resonated with a knowing of what I was feeling.

I started to lightly pluck the strings playing a duet with the wind. I then realized that if I moved my hand upwind from the harp it would change the music that the harp was playing. My hands were playing the wind as we both played the harp. I jumped up and started dancing with the wind and the rhythms and tones of the melody reverberated with my body's movement.

What started out to be a melancholy evening with my harp turned into a joyous party. While I was still feeling the exhilaration of this relationship, I made the drawing celebrating this music in the piece "The Wind Sang To Me."

(24 k gold, electrum, silver, star ruby, amethyst, opals, ivory, 1988)

BOANN

Sometimes, the inspirations for my designs come from my dreams and other times they come to the dreams of friends. This letter arrived one day from a Canadian grandmother and it motivated me to create the Tree Goddess piece.

"I had a dream and I think it's connected to-intended for you and Heyoka: the motherfigure Boann. I saw this tree-woman; the trunk of the tree was the body of the woman, her legs became the roots, her feet were still visible as feet but her toes were going into the earth. The limbs of the tree turned into the strands of her hair, her face was turned up a bit, she was looking into the tree, and I think she was watching birds. She had her hands/arms raised and her hair sort of went from being limbs, branches and leaves.

She's the figure who knew the secrets of navigation and mathematics and whose menstrual blood during her time as she was disguised as a tree, fell into the water, the salmon ate it, their flesh turned from white to red, and then the Celtic women caught the salmon, ate the flesh, and the secrets were given to them..."

(24k gold, silver, copper, sapphire, emerald, spinel, ivory, 1985)

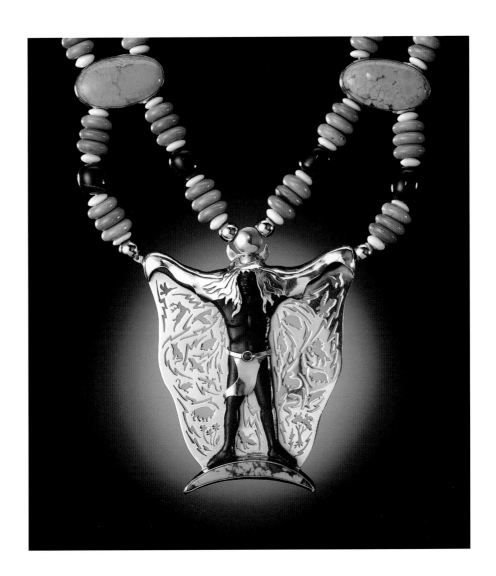

THUNDERING EARTH

The male energy power of the Earth is called, in the southwest, Thundering Earth. This archetypal spirit is the Nature God that is found in mythologies through out the world. Other names that he is known by are the Wild Man, Cernunnos, Dionysus, the Green Man, or the great god Pan. Much of the historical power of this myth was lost as he was diabolized by the emerging religions. Pan then became the popular image for the Devil.

With the loss of this archetype, the Earth has suffered ecological disasters as Nature and Her protector became an enemy to be conquered. To our ancestors, Pan did not cause "panic" when He was encountered. The Earth God was celebrated for his wild power and the way he protected our Mother Earth.

(24 k gold, electrum, silver, pipestone, emerald, turquoise, sugilite, 1989)

EPONA

On a green hillside near Uffington, England, there is the famous 370-foot chalk-cut image of the White Mare. A replica of this white horse is carved upon the shield of the Goddess in this necklace. Epona, goddess of the white horse was honored all over Europe. In Greece, she was the mare-headed Demeter whose destroyer aspect was the Black Mare or Nightmare. The Mare Goddess was the title applied to the queen of the Amazons, the Goddess worshiping tribes that held influence from North Africa to Northern Europe.

Ceremonies to Epona remained in England up to 1826, with Lady Godiva's naked ride through town on a white horse in the spring. In the Goddess's May-Eve procession, she would renew her virginity, consummate the sacred marriage, and provide the blessings of fertility for the coming year. In the nursery rhyme "Ride a Cock-Horse," she is called the "fine lady on the white horse."

On a trip to England, I visited this sacred sight with its bright, white chalk carving contrasting the brilliant green of the hills. At the bottom of the hill, facing toward this ancient white horse, is an earth pyramid. The top of the earth mound is flat with a white crescent moon carved into the grass. It was here that I chose to do my quiet ceremony celebrating the powers that remain to work through this sacred image of the Goddess.

After my honoring ceremony, a young man who lived nearby approached me and spoke of the local legends concerning the horse. It is told that St. George killed the dragon upon the earthen mound and the crescent carving was said to be a stain left by the dragon's blood where no grass would grow. Dragons represent the wisdom of the ancient mysteries and this legend speaks of some of the actual violent history surrounding this pyramid temple. He also told me an old tale: if you stand on the eye of the horse and turn around three times your wish will be granted. I asked if he had ever made such a wish and he answered, "Of course."

(24 k gold, electrum, silver, emerald, malachite, diamond, ivory, 1989)

ANUBIS

To the ancient Egyptians, the gate keeper of the world of our dreams is called Anubis. He is the sacred jackal who can find his way through the darkest night and leave a trail that we may follow by day. The super sensitive hearing and sense of smell that the Egyptian coyotes have may be a clue to the sensory organs that help us to find our way through the dark realms. Anubis can be our guide into the astral world of sleep and help us to remember the symbols that speak within our dreams.

Jackals are also carrion-eaters and are revered as a companion of the Goddess as receiver of the dead. In India, the goddess of life and death is Kali and her consort is Shiva, whose name means jackal. Likewise in Egypt, Anubis is the consort to Nephthys the under-world aspect of the goddess Isis.

Anubis is the god of mummification and the guide of souls after death. He is the messenger between the worlds of life and death. Every night as we enter the "little death" of sleep, Anubis can help us to make our conscious and subconscious become interactive. As our dream world is integrated more fully into our waking world, we may bring our lives into a more complete balance.

This small statue is kept near where I sleep as a helper in my nightly journeys through the world of sleep and dreams. The original was carved out of ebony wood and inlaid with 24 k gold as was the tradition in ancient Egypt. Later I made a mold of this carving and produced an edition in cast bronze.

(Ebony, 24 k gold, ivory, lapis, or bronze, limited edition 250, inlaid with
ivory and ebony, 1986. In the collection of Quincy Jones.)

ART FROM THE SACRED VOID
ASCENDING

At the time of this writing, I have lived here at Our Lady of the Lake for thirteen years. This is the longest time that I have ever lived in one place and I am starting to feel roots growing out of my feet and into this earth. Although I am rooted to the ground, my spirit soars with the eagles that have brought me some of their medicine power as they visit our land. Eagles fly the highest and have the best vision of all the world's creatures. One of their powers is to see the greater picture of the world and see the interrelationship of all things. As I live here, the overall view of my life comes more into perspective.

OJAI 1981

My adventures, experiences, and works of art are beginning to have meaning as parts of a puzzle that is my life. Much of my life has had the upward momentum of success and achievement. I may have stayed on this vertical ascent until I flamed out like a shooting star as many artists do. At one time, I was so busy excelling that I nearly missed many of the lessons that life was gifting me with. Some of these lessons were so painful that I had cut them off and at the same time cut off a part of myself.

As I worked to embrace the painful feelings that I disowned on my upward journey, I now tried to honor the grief and sadness that life had given to me. I tried to see that my grief and joy are like the opposite banks on the river of life. It was not my place to turn away from one of the banks, rather to surrender to the water's current. If I had trust in the river of life, I would flow by caressing both banks. From the source of creation, the stream would carry me back to the source of creation. The upward journey toward achievement was still celebrated although now I also honored the downward descent into introspection and the Sacred Void.

In honoring the downward spiral, there was a deeper understanding of my artistic process. I found that creating magical art is a birthing process which comes from the feminine part of myself. It is very much a Goddess energy. We may find the Goddess, who is sometimes called the door or gateway, within the Sacred Void.

The Sacred Womb of Creation, the Sacred Void, in psychology is also called the unconscious. Imagination, intuition and artistic inspiration are found within the void. A concept that one of our grandfathers has brought to us is that the conscious mind is like an island, with the unconscious being the surrounding ocean. Paintings, sculpture or jewelry can be created from the conscious mind, although for these objects to be magical art, the unconscious must be embraced.

As we enter the Sacred Void, we may touch all people and powers. This touching is sometimes called the collective unconscious and is thought to connect all of us. Symbols found in this place, that we incorporate into our art, are recognized by people around the world. These symbols or powers are called archetypes and they resonate for all of us. If I incorporated an eagle into a piece of jewelry, that symbol would evoke a similar feeling for an African, Australian, European or any other person who has experienced this animal power. When a Goddess is used as a mythical symbol, there is a part of us that has an understanding about the energy that has been called to the jewelry.

Art created by widely separated cultures throughout history have similarities that can be explained by a meeting within the collective unconscious. Artists from all times and places have received inspirations that are like branches from the same tree. The reason we have sought artistic expression is to try to embody our feelings and to find understanding in our life. Through art we can communicate emotions that are difficult to capture with words. Artistic creations explore the needs and impulses in life that we all share.

THE MYTHICAL IMAGE

In our mythological stories, there is an attempt to explain energies that are impossible to verbalize. The transcendent can be felt, however it is difficult to speak about. Through our myths and our art works we can talk about our feelings. We respond to archetypes because they can help us to understand the different energy centers in our body that combine to create the whole human. Mythical images are born so we may speak about these powers that are in conflict and how to bring them into balance. The archetypes are our gift from the Sacred Void that help us to understand how to become whole.

The shamans and storytellers in our ancient tribes were the keepers of our myths. Events in the stories would reflect different life passages as we mature and change throughout life. Myths evolved to help people see their place in Nature and their relationship to family and tribe. These oral stories were needed to keep balance within the tribe and within the individual. The shamans were also the artists of the tribe who created paintings and carvings to represent and hold the power of the myths. An important part in the telling of the stories were dances and masks. The myths were alive and grew and changed as the culture evolved.

Later, the myths were entrusted to priestesses and priests of the temples. The stories were written in temple texts and the sacred art became more elaborate. Even though the myths were written down, very few of the people were literate so art, stories and dance were still the principal means of passing the myths to the people. The dances and stories became sacred theater and were performed by the priestesses and priests. The plays were meant to create a catharsis in the audience, to touch their innermost emotional center and to teach them about life.

In our present time, the myths and archetypes are still seen in our films. The shero, hero, king, goddess of love and many others appear in our stories. From the quality and content in our films and other art forms, it appears that our present myth makers do not see their work as sacred. The archetypal images are mostly used to exploit their power for profit. The neurotic and selfish use of sacred images in modern works reflect the imbalances in our culture and in ourselves.

I realize that we cannot go back in history and totally embrace the ancient myths to bring balance to our lives. As artists we are the new myth-makers of our time. We have the responsibility to interpret the myths of our ancient grandparents and include the changes we have wrought in the world as humanity has evolved. When we look at the overwhelming problems in the world, we must admit that as myth makers we have failed. Most of our problems have arisen while battling to decide who's got the only right myth. When looking at other tribes, cultures, religions or nations we have searched for differences not similarities. If we celebrate the rich heritage of all cultures and see that all traditions evolved so that humanity would survive and prosper we may see the broader picture. While honoring the treasures that are inherent in all historical myths, we may ultimately create a global archetype. It is imperative that we embrace what our ancient teachers say: we are all related in one family.

If we as artists embrace the global view of humanity as one family our art will help to create the contemporary myth that we so desperately need. Our tribal myths evolved slowly over thousands of years throughout the history of humankind. When there was a deficiency in a culture, a myth would be born to help the people fulfill their needs. The mysteries of life could be woven into the myths in order to help a person live in harmony with themselves, their tribe and the environment. By looking at our collective problems, artists may find the healing myths needed to help bring us balance.

When the founding fathers of America were drafting our constitution, they borrowed many elements from the Iroquois Confederacy. This great confederation of tribes had a very enlightened government. They had one law which all other new laws must be measured against. That law was "every new law must be considered based on how it would effect the children for seven generations." As we recreate our myths it would be prudent to embrace this wise tradition from our ancestors. Each new myth may be viewed by how it will affect our children's children into the seventh generation.

As myth-makers we have only to look at what the signs in our cultures and in our environment are saying to us. The cultural and ecological cataclysms that are affecting us all will become our teachers. If we can learn from our mistakes, then we can heal the problems we have created. These signs speak to me of imbalance and any myths that I as an artist call into my pieces must work toward balance now and for all the future generations.

My art work draws from many cultures all over the world because I feel a strong attraction to many historical periods when the art reflected a golden age of human achievement. If we see our human family as all being related, then we can also embrace all ancestors as our own grandparents. With this view of the world, I can work within the style of ancient Egypt, Greece or Maya and still be working within my own personal tradition.

If I was raised in an isolated tribal culture, my art might have been confined to that culture. Since I was born into a mixed culture and have in my ancestry mixed races it feels comfortable for me to embrace a more eclectic view in my work. I love ethnic art and like to see the strong traditional ties in a creation and to feel the ancient magnetism in a piece. Artists that have strong racial and cultural purity have a wonderful gift from their grandparents. For most of us who live in our mass media-dominated world, it is difficult for us not to be influenced by other cultures. As world artists we may honor our roots while celebrating our global family and its future as we conjure art from the Sacred Void.

MESSENGER OF THE SKY

Eagles often visit our land here and sometimes they leave us a token, one of their feathers. One of the indigenous people's names for this great being is wing flapper. Although the silhouette of an eagle and hawk are very similar from a distance, the characteristic wing movement of eagle is easy to distinguish. The eight foot wing span makes its movement appear to be in slow motion or possibly in another time dimension. When watching an eagle fly, sometimes I am carried into a quiet stillness similar to the place I experience in meditation.

When an Eagle appears to a medicine person, this encounter has more meaning than the mere physical beauty of flight. This meeting is called a Sweet Medicine Gift, and adds significance to the thoughts, feelings, or ceremony of the moment.

(24k gold, silver ebony, lapis lazuli,
moonstones, diopsite, ivory, 1985)

TURQUOISE LADY

HATHOR

GODDESS OF HEAVEN

Hathor is the Egyptian Goddess of Heaven. Her name means womb and Horus (the Sun). Like the Wakan or Sacred Void of the Native Americans, she and her sacred twin, the Divine Serpent, existed before creation. The Egyptian hieroglyph for the word Goddess is the cobra. Hathor created Heaven and Earth and all life. She is also patroness of music, dancing, and the teacher of sexual ecstasy.

In her aspect of the huntress she is called Hathor-Sekmet, the lionheaded Goddess, the Sphinx. As well as Creatress, she is the Destroyeress, a necessary force to cause the turning of the cycles. Hathor is called the Lady of the Sycamore and this tree is the living body of Hathor on Earth. To eat of the sycamore fig tree is to eat the flesh and fluid of the Goddess. It is through the sacred tree that we can approach the Goddess to honor and learn from her.

The Egyptian Goddess Isis is sometimes called "Lady of Turquoise." To certain Native American peoples, the First Mother was also called "Turquoise Lady." She was the Queen of Heaven and the sacred womb of the sky. As the Great Goddess she gave birth to the two legged: humans; the four legged: animals; the winged: birds; the standing people: trees; and the ancient ones: stones.

She created the stone turquoise to reflect the color of her own heavenly body — the sky. In turquoise, the magic of her body is given as a gift to the earth and, as seen from space, the world is a turquoise-blue sphere.

The magic of turquoise is celebrated all over the world. Turquoise means "Turkish stone" and the Turks called it the lucky stone. It is said that wearing turquoise will protect one from injuries resulting from falls. For this reason, the Tibetans, Persians and Turks attached turquoise to the bridles of their horses to make them sure-footed.

Buddhists say that Buddha destroyed a monster with the help of a turquoise stone. Turquoise has the property of changing colors and in Arabia this quality will warn of approaching danger. In Europe, the fading color may foretell bad health.

It is said that turquoise has more power when received as a gift, and to gain good luck and fortune, the wearer should look upon a turquoise immediately after first seeing the new moon.

("Turquoise Lady" 24 k gold, silver, electrum, carved turquoise,
emerald, mother-of-pearl, quartz crystal, 1992)

("Hathor" 24 k gold, electurm, silver, copper, turquoise,
apis lazuli, coral, ebony, bone, black onyx, 1985)

OSA

PELE

Volcano Goddesses

From the beginning of time, volcanos have been worshipped by the people. They are seen as doorways into the Great Mother. In the fiery cauldrons of her womb she regenerates the dead. The dead are said to live on in the fire of the volcanos, never dying but in a state of bliss until they are reborn.

In Europe, the volcano goddess who kept the souls of the dead was called Hel. She was absorbed into the christian mythology and she became the fiery realm of hell. In this later mythology the souls were no longer in bliss and her realm became a place of punishment and eternal doom. As the pagan deities were diabolized, some medieval authorities declared that volcanos were entrances to eternal punishment.

The ancestral fire goddess in Japan is called Mother Fuji. People still make pilgrimages to her holy body, the volcano Fujiyama.

In Mother Africa, the volcano goddess is called Osa. She is a dynamic goddess who creates storms when she ruffles her skirts. When she uses her whip, she causes thunder and lightning. Snakes are her animal powers and her hair is the rainbow.

In Hawaii, where all the earth that rises above the ocean is of volcanic origin, the volcano goddess is called Mother Pele. She also keeps the souls of the dead in her volcanic afterworlds. It is said that sometimes she walks along secluded roads as an old wise woman with long flowing white hair. If we stop to give her a ride, we are inviting the Goddess herself into our circle. A friend of mine who has long white hair and lives on Hawaii said that when she walks the back country roads, many of the local people are afraid of her.

("Osa" 24 k gold, electrum, silver, copper, carved ebony,
yellow sapphire, ruby, sugilite, citrine, smokey quartz, 1987)

("Pele" 24 k gold, electrum, silver, copper,
rubies, carved pipestone, 1992)

EARTH MOTHER

**(Bronze, 11 inches, 1981, limited edition of 25.
In the collection of Yogi Bhajan.)**

SKY FATHER

**(Bronze, 18 inches, 1981, limited edition of 25.
In the collection of Christopher Lambert and Elton John.)**

EARTH FATHER

(Bronze, 14 inches, 1985, limited edition of 25)

SKY MOTHER

(Bronze, 19 inches, 1985, limited edition of 25)

CREATIVE FIRE
THE PASSION

When I return from the Sacred Void with an idea that wants to become a work of art it is like a spark of inspiration. Somehow this spark needs to be become a raging fire in order to be manifested. Many people who have connected with the source of creation and have come back with a vision, let it fade into forgetfulness. The vision needs to be nurtured to become the fire that turns into passion. Passion has a life of its own and together we create the work of art. I am not controlling the creative process, I am merely a part of something much greater than myself.

The inspiration is like a seed and the artist is like a gardener. The apple seed has the tree sleeping within its genetic memory. As a gardener I would not worry about the seed's potential to be a tree. My place would be to nurture the seed so that it could manifest its own life potential. I can't force a seed to become a tree and as an artist I cannot force my vision into completion. The artistic inspiration is not my slave, it is my helper and my companion.

Often, as I am working on a piece and am getting too linear in my thinking about how the finished art work will look, something will seemingly go wrong. There may be a crack, a melt-down or some other disaster will happen to it. At that point the piece is usually not ruined, it will merely change and evolve in another direction. Many times the new direction will bring the piece into a more beautiful or innovative expression. My artist friends sometimes call these misadventures "happy accidents." I am not sure I believe in accidents and to me the life of the piece is working with me in its creation.

The creative inspiration is an awesome, sometimes consuming energy. Energetically, the artistic impulse originates in the same body center as passion, rage, creativity, sexuality and survival. As we create, we are in contact with extraordinary primal powers. These powers feel to me very similar to the energies that I was dancing with as I ran in my gang in East L A.

Even as a teenager I was following artistic pursuits. My art work at the time mostly decorated our lowrider cars. The other members of the Essexs seemed to suffer much more disastrous consequences from our impulses of that time than I did . I feel that having an artistic outlet during adolescence and other times in my life helped me through my life's passages. There are many times in my life that I am not sure that I could have survived had it not been for my artistic expression. As I have nurtured my visions into the material world, the Muses have nurtured me through my sometimes devastating experiences.

For me the finishing of a work of art or the sale of it is often not the goal of the piece. Actually, the finished piece often feels anti-climactic to the process of creating it. When I have worked passionately on a sculpture for weeks, there is a depression upon its completion. It is hard to describe although it feels similar to the ending of a relationship with a loved one. The joy, pain, doubt and ecstasy of the working relationship comes to an end. The process of working on the sculpture is my reward and my bliss.

Much of humanity seems to be caught up in the belief that work is drudgery. Work is seen as something we have to do for survival or some other future goal. Since we spend most of our lives working, it seems natural that we need to choose what brings us our greatest joy to be our life's work. We cannot own a reward that is in the future — we can only possess what is in the present. If we do not love our work we are denying ourselves one of life's greatest gifts. Personally, it is hard for me to imagine what my life would have been like had I not chosen to be my work that which is my bliss.

My other primary passion is striving to embrace the fullness of my life's potential. This passion has led me to ceremony, mythology, spirituality and also back again to my art work. It is impossible for me to separate my art work from my pursuit of becoming a whole human. Every aspect of my life and the world around me is there to teach me more about who I am and my place in the world. If I do not live life to its fullness, I feel I am not honoring the gift of life that the universe has provided.

As I pursue the fullness of life and my passion of the moment, the inspirations for my work come in unexpected ways. This story of how one of my inspirations came to me may better illustrate my creative process. Our journey will take us in many directions and eventually bring us back to the pieces and their origin.

At midsummer, on the ancestral land of the Crow People, I was in a Sundance ceremony. A round lodge was built, open to the sky above and in the center of the lodge was the sundance tree. While fasting food and water, the women and men in this lodge danced to the tree for three days and nights.

The Montana sun was scorching on the third day during the healing ceremony and I felt sick and unable to stand let alone dance. In ancient times, there was a live eagle tethered to the limb of the tree although now we use a stuffed eagle. Looking at this eagle in the sundance tree I was able to stand. The energy of the eagle danced in and through me. Without noticing the 110 degree heat I danced my strongest dance of the ceremony. When an animal power comes to a dancer it is an awesome relationship. To me this was a miraculous encounter and the sculpture "Sky Father" speaks more clearly of this magical moment than the preceding words.

Getting started — that can be a problem. I am good friends with some of the members of the Beatles, and when John Lennon was killed I was devastated. In a state of deep depression, I wanted to do something as beautiful as this senseless killing was ugly. Depression is just another form of energy. We may let it immobilize us or we can use this energy to fuel our creativity. I thought of my eagle vision and started my first drawing.

The drawing surprised me when it turned out to be the archetypal image of Sky Father as portrayed in many cultures throughout history. Being very committed to working toward a sacred balance, I knew that if I made Sky Father I must make Earth Mother. Since I work in ceremony with the sacred pipe, and she is very precious to me, I decided to use White Buffalo Woman as Earth Mother. In looking at the drawings, I saw that I was creating a medicine wheel with Sky Father in the east and Earth Mother in the west. Several years were to pass before the directions of north and south were to make themselves known to me.

During the time that the inspiration for Sky Mother was dawning, I was working with a sundance sister who was very much a warrioress-amazon type person. She told me that she felt more like Sky Father who is active and dynamic than Earth Mother who is quiet and meditative. It was not my intention to be sexually biased in doing the directions east and west although from this teaching I understood the importance of balancing the wheel in the directions of north and south. The vision of Sky Mother took shape as the winged First Mother, the Sacred Void. I could envision First Mother in the north with the lightning bolts of the first spark of life flashing from her wings. I could not see the sculpture that would be in the south, and did not feel I could start on Sky Mother until the vision of the wheel was complete.

In the Southwest, sitting under a starry sky, with lightning dancing in all directions, three medicine sisters and myself were sitting in ceremony. We were building a circle of power for the healing of the earth. This was very much a Goddess ceremony and I thought we had created a balanced wheel when an unexpected guest came to our ceremony. One of the women in the circle, using her mediumship ability, informed us that someone wanted to speak to us.

He was an archetypal power whose name was Thundering Earth and his booming voice was in a rage for not being invited to the circle. There was a chill that ran up my back, as I felt very much like a young apprentice magician who had blundered. He told us that without him to guard her, the Goddess would not have a protected place in which to work her magic of birthing. There was a buffalo skull by the sweatlodge and I picked it up and placed it in our circle. I spoke to the Earth Father or as he is sometimes called the Horned God and celebrated his coming to our circle.

Later, in honor of Thundering Earth I was designing a piece of jewelry (see page 71). When the drawing was finished I saw looking back at me the missing sculpture I was searching for to be in the south of the Medicine Wheel. The piece of jewelry was set aside and I immediately started work on the two new sculptures.

The completion of this medicine wheel of sculptures took several years and I learned a great deal about my personal symbols in the process. The wheel is also a reflection of my personal growth during these years and a voice from the archetypes that spoke through me (see sculptures on pages 84, 85, 86, 87).

The creative experence is wonderful although it is not necessarily kind or gentle. After the completion of a sculpture, I am exhausted and drained. While dancing with the Muses of inspiration and the archetypal powers, my physical and personal needs are often forgotten. The Muses do not seem to have much understanding of human needs and limitations. Artists often die a young death as they are consumed in the creative inspirational flame. Artistic inspiration sometimes feels more like a tumultuous love affair along with the accompanying pain, passion and ecstasy. The Muse that is a part of me for a while, is annoyed by any interruption, even by someone I love. Over the years I have learned to form disciplines that bring me back to Earth as I spend weeks working on a piece.

Meditation, regular healthy meals, Yoga exercises and long walks in the woods help to ground me after being in the other worldly dimensions of the creative universe. Paying close attention the needs of my loved ones helps me stay connected to my humanity as well. It takes constant awareness on my part and a lot of understanding from my partner to stay bonded in a relationship. Without my physical strength or my supportive friends, I would not have the power nor the will to do the demanding creative work.

ORNAMENT GALLERY, SANTA FE, 1993

The nurturing Goddess of life is also the destroying Goddess of death. Along with the bliss of being a creative artist there is the sacrifice. The pain and suffering associated with the work are all part of the process and necessary for the wholeness of a work of art. If I were to run from the pain involved in the creative process, I would not be able to fully embrace the life of an artist.

As I sit here working with Maxine, my computer, I can look out at the forest and lake shimmering in the sunlight. There was a light snow last night and I long to go cross country skiing in the fresh powder like I did yesterday. However I know that to have the respect and help of the Muses while writing this story I need to be disciplined and sit here working today. There have been many greater sacrifices over the years than missing a day of skiing, and some of these sacrifices hold painful memories for me. When I look back over my life, the sacrifices have been balanced by the bliss of being in the creative fire.

GRANDMOTHER NORTH MAKING SNOW

To the indigenous peoples of the North American plains, there is a color and power given to each of the four cardinal directions. Yellow is to the east, red is the color of the south, to the west is black and white is the north, whose aspect is wisdom.

These same people called Canada, Grandmother's Land. Living near the border to Grandmother's Land, we can feel the immense brooding power from the north. Much of her power seems to come from the fact that humans have impacted this land less than other parts of the world. Her ancient natural rhythms are still evident.

"Grandmother North Making Snow" was created as the first taste of winter was felt in the north winds of late fall. With the mountains we can see in Grandmother's Land turning white, comes the knowlege she may soon blanket our home in snow. Due to global warming and the shifting of seasons, she has touched us very lightly with winter the past several years. The loss of winter is affecting our lives drastically, especially our trees.

With pollution and increased radiation as the ozone layer decreases, our forests are dying at an alarming rate. The natural immunity of the trees can no longer fight off the diseases that attack the forest. At one time, Grandmother North gave a us a strong helping hand as she held us in the cold grip of winter. Her cold would help control the insects that are killing the trees. Although Her touch often seems harsh, the beauty of Grandmother North with her snow, held wisdom and balance. When we did the ceremony of "waking up" this necklace, Grandmother North came to our celebration — we walked outside and the first snow was falling.

(24K, silver, electrum, sapphires, diamonds , star quartz, opal, 1992)

QUETZALCOATL

Coatl is the sacred snake whose movements mirror the way that Kundalini energy moves up the spinal column awakening the wheels of light that surround each of the major body centers. When this serpentine energy reaches the crown chakra at the top of the head, we are one with the Universal. Quetzal is the sacred bird that connects Earthly power with the Heavily realms of the universe. Together the Quetzal and the Coatl are the creatures that are closest to the earth and heaven as well as representing the sacred balance of female and male.

This is the teaching within the name Quetzalcoatl, the teacher / savior deity to the Mayan and other Mexican peoples. According to Mayan tradition, this deity returns at specific times to again instruct humanity. According to the Mayan calendar, we are again in the time when Quetzalcoatl will return, and many people are expecting a savior to rescue us from all our problems.

The last time that a date in the Mayan calendar said that Quetzalcoatl would appear is the exact day that Cortez arrived in Mexico. Many indigenous people accepted him as the savior although he became a destroyer who raped and pillaged his way across the New World. Within one generation this supposed savior had destroyed the great cultures of Mexico along with 95 percent of the population.

At the top of this buckle is the symbol that will herald the coming of this deity , the morning star or the planet Venus. The Mayans say that the savior will come from the East like the shining star. I feel since Venus is the Goddess of love, that "love" will proclaim the coming of the balanced, awakened teacher.

For me, Quetzalcoatl is a power that is awakening within every human at this time. If we look inward instead of outward for a savior, we all have the potential to become the winged serpent.

(Silver, 24k gold, electrum, brass, copper, emerald, diopsite, 1992)

CREATIVE SPIRAL SHIELD

Spirals appear the world over and they are one of the oldest and most sacred of symbols. It represents a human's cyclic journey that leads to the center of the wheel of life. Most often the journey is into the labyrinth or underworld to be reborn.

The source of this design is the Hopi Rain Bird Spirit. It is the spiral movement of creation incorporating all the elements which bring forth life. This spiral is reflected throughout Nature, including the DNA spiral molecules, building blocks of life. The bird designs in Rain Bird Shield are reflections of the spiral movement within thunder clouds. The wind's motion sends out wisps of clouds that look like eagle heads around the edges of the clouds.

This necklace is my personal shield, and as I often do, I have a different design on both sides of the shield. On the reverse side is Jaguar Priestess, another power that I work with. The Rain Bird side is more reflective and protective and the priestess side is introspective, so that side is turned out during ceremony.

(24 k gold, electrum, silver, lapis lazuli, jet, turquoise, malachite,
coral, mother of pearl, quartz, diamond, emerald, pipestone, sugilite, bone, 1985)

CEREMONIAL ART
MAKING A CIRCLE

I feel that the abundance of all the gifts that life brings to us leaves us so full that we need to find a way to complete a circle of giving. If we become a dam in the river of life, the water from the source cannot flow through us. An important lesson that I have learned from tribal peoples is to give back to the universe by doing ceremony.

A ceremony is an action that celebrates the powers that bring us life. It may be as simple as pausing to honor a sunrise, knowing that all life on Earth owes its survival to the sun. Ceremony sometimes is extremely complicated and can last for days until we become so tired and worn out that our brain can be silent for a while. At this point we may break through to another part of our self that is usually hidden and honor life in a more connected way.

OUR LADY OF THE LAKE 1985

As a young boy I was taught to pray to the creator in thankfulness. Often as I listened to myself or to the members of my father's church, it seemed that the prayers happened mostly in the intellect and did not unite us with God. An old deacon in the Baptist Church expressed it clearly one time. He said, "sometimes our prayers feel like they don't get past the roof."

There were a few ancient ceremonies that were still alive in the old church of my youth. The communion ceremony especially made me feel connected to spirit and to the sacrifice of the Christ to life. Later the Native American ceremonies that I participated in helped me to feel an even stronger connection to the source of all life. I did not reject my family's traditional religion, rather it became a part of a much larger whole. I now see that the myths of all our traditions speak about the Creator/Creatoress and our place within the universe. They all have a place on the wheel of life and have something to teach us.

OFFERINGS

A few days ago when I was writing about something an apprentice had written to me in a letter I went to my file cabinet. The file was missing and I looked through every drawer and then throughout my studio. In the European traditions when we lose something they say it was the fairies. They say that if we forget to give the fairies an offering of food they will play tricks on us. These offerings of food are a way of thanking the spirits that live in plants, trees, stones, springs and in other facets of Nature. In certain ceremonies such as the sweat lodge, we leave such an offering for the nature elementals. The sweat lodge was still under the snow of winter when the file was lost and our last offering had been in the autumn. I was thinking of doing another one soon when suddenly the file appeared in the middle of my desk. Without questioning what, where or why, I took an offering of food outside to the nature spirits. Later I found out that Katherine had a part in this magic when she found the file behind the desk and placed it on top.

Actions speak louder than words. This is especially true in a world where truth is bent in order to win in the games that we often play in life. When honesty is undervalued, words do not mean very much. The ceremony of the giving of food and tea are a much more meaningful gift than a simple thanks. I know that after this offering, the fairies have an understanding that I appreciate them for all the help they bring to humankind. Also, I hope not to lose anything else in the near future.

The reason that I know that sacrificial offerings are acknowledged is that the spirits sometimes respond with eloquence and beauty. Grandmother Mahad'yumi had asked me to help her in the building of a medicine wheel in the mountains where she smoked her pipe. With the help of several medicine sisters and brothers, we spent two days laboring on the wheel of stones. The ceremony started at night while we aligned the four direction spokes of the wheel with the north star. It was in the middle of summer and, during the last part of the ceremony, we were hot, dirty and sweaty. What had started out to be a small circle of stones looked more like a miniature Stonehenge. As we were waking up the wheel, I was calling in the four elements of creation.

The wheel was near a stream under the protection of oak trees that shaded us from the still hot summer day. I spoke to the elements: "sacred fire of creation we call you to this circle", as I burned a few dry leaves in the center of the medicine wheel — "water of healing we need you here", while water was poured onto the fire — "element of the life-giving earth we celebrate you", and dirt was poured on top of the other two — "sacred element of air we honor the gift of your.........(As I reached for the flowers that represented the air elemental I realized that I had forgotten them. My medicine brother Hawk who was helping me saw my predicament and handed me his red tail fan to symbolize the air. I lifted the fan and was about to finish my sentence with "your breath of life" when the stillness of the dry air was broken by a strong wind. Everyone around the wheel sighed at once as the cool breeze danced around us shaking all the leaves on the trees above us.).........music". A few years later our wise old grandmother's ashes were scattered around this medicine wheel that had such a loving relationship with her.

Within ceremonies, I always try to leave room for the unexpected event for often it is the most magical part of a ceremony. If I am too attached to a written or ritualistic form of a ceremony it may exclude certain powers that want to come and help me. Last summer, as I was performing a wedding ceremony along the coast of Northern California, we had an uninvited guest. We were in an ancient cypress grove on the cliffs overlooking the ocean. As we smoked the pipe and called the powers of the land to join us, a crow lit in the tree above us and started to squawk at us. Our rehearsed plan was momentarily halted as we talked to the crow thanking her for coming to the wedding. It was a beautiful ceremony, however the part that people will remember most will be the crow. I work at being very alert when in ceremony for the magic that is often subtle and elusive.

Often as I read books by various medicine people the stories they tell are so fantastic that I wonder if they have occurred in this dimension. Sometimes these stories sound like they have taken place in the world of the imagination. I enjoy a good story as much as anyone, however, I wonder if these fantastic stories give too grand an expectation to young people as they are learning to do ceremony. When I first started doing ceremony, I was disappointed because something monumental never happened. Later I realized that the most insignificant occurrence was magical if I was awake enough to the present moment to notice it.

Once a friend of mine went to a gathering of people in the Southwest. Someone had a vision that White Buffalo Woman was going to return on a certain day at a particular place in the mountains. There were many people there for this great event although nothing seemed to be happening. My medicine brother was sitting looking out at the mountains when he noticed that a patch of snow on the mountain across the valley was shaped like a buffalo. He tried to go around and tell everyone about it but they were too busy waiting for something spectacular to happen and they ignored him. He returned to his spot and meditated on the White Buffalo and was probably the only one there for whom the prophecy was a reality.

As I work at my bench, I know that, if I intend for the jewelry to be protective or healing, something will happen to the piece. The powers that are called by my intent will change the life force within the jewelry. I also understand that if I keep a close relationship with the powers that they will be more responsive with their help. Like all beings, the powers do not like to be controlled or taken for granted. They are free, not slaves, so the way that I show my appreciation and respect is by honoring them in ceremony.

When I design a ceremony I treat it like an art piece that I am creating. I work to create beauty, symmetry, rhythm, power and purpose. The energy that I am working with is sculpted and molded as if I were making a work of art. My sacred pipe is included to call in all the energies of the universe and to help me to enter into the meditative stillness of being. Specific powers that are necessary for the full potential of the piece to be realized are honored.

A waking up or conjuring ceremony for my jewelry will include the four elements of life: fire, water, earth and air. The moon and the sun are invited into the circle of magic. There are different counts and systems that can be used when calling the heavenly spheres. Alchemists used a seven count and worked with the visible planets. The Vedic system of astrology may be used or several other disciplines from diverse traditions. No matter what name is used, the planetary powers will recognize that we are calling them to the medicine object. Different systems of numerology or the sacred meaning of numbers can be woven into the art piece or into the ceremony.

The finished pieces are placed on my altar which is a small round table in a secluded room used only for ceremonial purposes. On the table stands a sculpture depicting my personal vision the Goddess (see page 28). She is a symbol of the life force that is the gifted to us by the Great Goddess. The statue helps me to remember that all the elemental and planetary powers come to us through this archetype.

I burn sweet grass to purify the energy in the room and the pieces on the altar. There are special objects and vestments that I wear only in ceremony that are put on while I work in conjuring. My eagle and condor feathers are held in my hand and then the art pieces are touched as I speak to the powers that have come to the magical circle. To the best of my ability, I stay centered, focused, honest and sincere. If we are doing a sweat lodge or Sundance around the time of the waking up ceremony, I will then hang the jewelry pieces on the sacred tree.

Over ten years ago a small forked stick of red willow was pushed into the ground in front of my sweat lodge. My sacred pipe was placed within the fork with the stem pointing toward the lodge during ceremony. It stayed alive sending out roots and growing into a forked tree that is now nearly forty feet tall. The willow tree became the center of our sundance ceremonies and I have developed a very close relationship with her over the years. The tree, like my statue, embodies the manifestation of life force coming to us from the Great Goddess. Our sundance tree is an immense help in charging the jewelry pieces with life.

The ceremony does not end with the jewelry and sculpture pieces being sold or given to a new keeper. In order for the magical art piece to express its full potential, the new overseer will want to continue with the ceremony. The protective quality of a piece may absorb the unbalanced energy that comes near it, therefore this unwanted energy needs to be cleaned from the Medicine object. There are several ways to do the cleaning ceremony, although our intent is the most important element. Sweetgrass or incense smoke is a good way to keep the energy pure around an object. Tying the piece to a tree that we have established a friendship with is very helpful. If the tree is a stranger to us then in the traditional way we leave tobacco or food as an offering to the tree for her help.

The more attention that we give our relationship with a power object the better it will work for us. As we feel refreshed after taking a shower, a medicine object feels renewed after our ceremony. When we work in ceremony with a magical object it becomes part of us and we part of it. As we develop a close rapport with the piece, it becomes a focus of our own personal power and the powers that come to us from the universe.

FAERIE CROWN

In my view of Nature, each tree, plant or flower has a spirit living within it. This spirit is the consciousness that sleeps within the seed and guides the growth of the plant throughout its life. The importance of these beings has been recognized by people throughout history.

They are called by many names: little people, sprites, devas, faeries. These little people live in the world of light that parallels our world. They are very sensitive to our thoughts and feelings. When they choose to show themselves to humans, the faeries reflect much of the person's own projected power and imagination. Often they are seen to have butterfly wings, although they do not need physical wings to fly.

(Silver, moonstones, emeralds, quartz crystal, 1976)

103

Ocean Mother

Whales are the ancient grandparents of the oceans and they keep the records of all earth's histories. Each year the whale's song changes along with the transitions that are taking place within the world. They sing their epic songs to all the water creatures and when we venture into their element the haunting music speaks to our very cellular memory.

Off the coast of Maui the humpback whales come every year in the wintertime. A medicine sister and I had taken a small rubber raft tour that takes people out to get a close look at the whales. As we floated in the ocean, the humpbacks came from all directions, two to four at a time, during the entire three hours of the trip. The guide said he had never seen the whales take such an interest in their boat, as they swam around the little raft waving their flippers at us.

While describing their music, the guide said that if we wanted to go swimming, we would hear the singing while diving under the water. At the time, I was thinking about how I had not brought an offering of tobacco with me to give to the whales. I was about to give to the ocean the necklace I was wearing. The give-away ceremony was forgotten when the guide said we could go into the water — I jumped.

I have often swam along the seashore. However, jumping into the sea, miles from shore was like jumping into the Sacred Void. The ocean seemed to glow with an energy that made my whole body tingle. I seemed to hear the music of the whales more with my body than with my ears. When I surfaced for air I realized that I had made my giveaway to this magical moment. In my excitement, I had forgotten to take off my sunglasses and had given them to the ocean.

When I designed the necklace "Ocean Mother," I worked to express the feeling I had swimming in the ocean with the whales: the intricately balanced water world of Mother Ocean with her children swimming all around her. At the bottom of the sacred shield is a barracuda enjoying my give-away; he's wearing my Serengeti's.

(24 k gold, electrum, silver, sapphires, moonstones, mother-of-pearl, iolite, 1987)

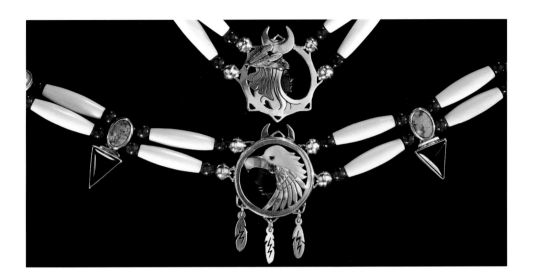

WHITE BUFFALO WOMAN

Long ago two young men were crossing the plains in the center of the land they called Turtle Island which we now have named America. They saw a person approaching them from a distance, and soon they could see a beautiful woman dressed in decorated white buckskin.

The first young man said that surely this is a sacred being to appear in this manner in the middle of the prairie. The second young man said that he had never seen such a beautiful woman, and he wanted to make love with her. He approached her and when he grew near a cloud enveloped them both.

She took the second young man in her arms and they went off and lived their life together. Their life was rich and full, however death eventually separated them. To the first young man the cloud lasted for only a moment, when it evaporated there was only the beautiful woman with a pile of bones at her feet.

He said, "You have come in a sacred manner, what would you have me do?" She told him to return to the village, have a medicine lodge put up in the center and she would come and be a teacher to the people. When the lodge was finished, she came into it holding a pipe in her hands.

She taught them to honer all the universe when tobacco is put into the pipe. The pipe was to be an altar and the center of their ceremonies. When the ceremony and teaching was complete, she gave the pipe to a medicine person and then returned onto the prairie. As the people were watching her walk away, she turned into a white buffalo and continued walking toward the horizon. The pipe and White Buffalo Woman's teachings brought peace and prosperity to the people.

On the reverse of this shield is "Eagle Dreamer." This eagle kachina dancer is touching the Great Spirit by joining with the eagle power. While White Buffalo Woman connects us to the Earth, Eagle Dreamer unites us with the Sky.

(Silver, 24k gold, electrum, pipestone, bone, emerald, lapis lazuli, turquoise, black onyx, 1990. In the collection of Tom Petty.)

THE ANIMAL POWERS
AWAKENING TO POWER

CHAPTER 10

Our ancestors lived in a very integrated way with the natural world and they had an especially close relationship with the animal powers. With a vast majority of our human family living in urban environments, we have imprisoned the animals in our zoos and our neighbors have become other humans. Living in our cities we have lost our connection with the animals that we once depended upon for our survival and our ceremonial life. Although we have separated ourselves from animalkind, our genetic memory still remembers these powers that have helped to shape humanity. Something wakes up in us when we see the wild animals on TV or when we go backpacking in the wilderness, because our social experiment of city life represents only a very small part of the history of humankind.

If our vision of ourselves includes only the world of our cities, we are missing a treasure that we have inherited from our ancestors. The animal powers sleep within us and if we reach out to them they will awaken and empower our life. As I embraced these powers, I found a great helper on my path toward becoming a whole human.

Since I have embodied the way that our ancestors saw the world, I consider all animals to be my relations. We are all children of life and are meant to share the world and learn to live in balance together. In the tribal traditions, each animal has a gift that they bring to the wheel of life. If we observe them closely, we can learn how the animals view the world and see how there are parts of ourselves that view the world from a similar perspective.

JAGUAR

Our grandparents teach us that there is a personal animal power that especially effects the way we perceive the world. The knowledge and wisdom of that animal is reflected in our personality traits and in our body language. An individual may be a bear person, deer person or any other animal may be their medicine animal. When it was first suggested to me that I had the medicine of a jaguar, it seemed very strange to me. I then reflected on how I walked through the forest and realized how feline my movements were.

In the larger sphere of my life, there are several other animals that have become my helpers as I develop an ever closer relationship with Nature. As I mentioned earlier in the book, the eagle medicine power is very strong for me at this time in my life. My friends agree that the cat medicine is easily seen in my mannerisms, although I now wonder about how eagle applies to my body language — perhaps it means that we both have rather large beaks.

In learning to work with the animal powers, they bring me much wisdom. As a closer relationship is developed with animalkind, they come more often to my dreams, visit my ceremonies and want to be in my art pieces. If I look at the particular animal's gift that has appeared to me then its medicine can become a way for nature to speak to me. If a snake comes to me, it can say something about the power of healing and rebirth. When a snake sheds its skin, it is like a rebirth, for its skin and body are forever young. The appearance of snake in my walks, my dreams or my ceremonies may be a message from life, awakening me to one of life's mysteries during this auspicious meeting.

When the pressures of being in college became too overwhelming, I would escape to the wilderness near Tecate, Mexico for the weekend. I was discovering a new way of walking along the trails of the brush covered hills. I was absorbed with meditating while I walked and the environment was responding to my aura. This process was making me feel more like a member of the surrounding flora and fauna instead of an alien intruder. On this hot summer day, I felt so connected to Nature that I was in complete harmony with my surroundings. I sensed something nearby and, looking around, I saw a huge rattlesnake a few feet away.

As a young boy, my teachers had told me that rattlesnakes were killers so when I had encountered one in the past I had smashed it with boulders. That day I felt no fear and the snake seemed to accept my being close to it for it did not coil up and rattle its tail. Sitting on the ground, I watched the snake as she slowly crawled by next to me. The patterns of her scales were like a beautiful tapestry while her movements were so graceful that they were mesmerizing. It was an incredible experience for me and I started to question all that I had learned about how dangerous snakes are.

All day long I thought about the snake and how it was on a trail that led to a friend's cabin. I wondered if he would be in danger and I wondered if I was negligent in my manly duties by not killing the rattlesnake.

Finally, I decided to kill the snake. Holding a large boulder I returned along the trail. The returning hike was the exact opposite of the earlier tranquil walk. I was full of fear and every sound made me jump and my heart pound. The same trail that had seemed so nurturing and embracing was now threatening and scary. I did not have to encounter this snake again to learn the lesson of how the two different ways of viewing Nature affected the way I felt on my walk in the wilderness.

A few years later a similar lesson was given to me. I was gathering dried yucca plants for my booth at the Renaissance fair and I was in a happy peaceful mood. It was against the rules to be in the hills surrounding the fair and one of the officials yelled at me to return. I was feeling so good that I felt a rush of hot anger surge through my body and I fully intended to yell back an insulting profanity. There was no chance to yell for my anger materialized in front of me. Feeling my energy, a rattlesnake shot out of the yucca with its mouth open and fangs bared. It left me with no doubt that wild creatures are sensitive to our emotions as the jaws snapped shut where I had been standing — having just executed a world class backwards standing broad jump.

COUNTING COUP

Over the years I have continued to develop this way of relating to Nature and it has brought me many magical and amusing encounters. I have found that if I sit still for a few hours, slowing down my breathing and concentrating on blending with Nature the forest will accept me and the wild creatures will continue their daily routines. I know I am accepted when the small animals approach close to me while they continue feeding. The first time a small bird landed on me it startled me and I scared it away. The next time I was more prepared and reveled in the magic of the moment although sometimes I wondered if they did not see me and I had become invisible.

Once, after meditating for a while in the forest, I noticed a hunter walking toward me. He appeared to be hunting rabbits as I watched his searching gaze and leveled shotgun. I expected him to say "Hi," though he seemed not to see me so I decided to speak first. I have noticed in the past, when I am practicing my silent walking, I sometimes encounter someone on the trail. If I do not speak, and they do not see me until I am a few inches away, they almost jump out of their skin. I then realized that I was in danger if the safety was off on the hunter's shotgun. It might go off in my direction if he was startled. With slow-centered breathing , I sat still in plain sight of him, ten feet from the trail, as he walked by.

Sometimes I will play the game of stalking and counting coup on the wild creatures. If I see an animal before I am seen then the game can begin. When I am downwind, most animals cannot sense me if I stand still. They are usually occupied with eating or stalking some other critter as I silently walk toward them. When they look up I freeze, for sometimes a very long time, until they forget what made them look up and start feeding again. Sometimes they will pretend to feed and quickly raise their head to try to trick me into moving. This may go on for an hour or more although sometimes I blow it by laughing. On different occasions I could have touched bobcats, rabbits, coyotes, muskrats and other small animals and have been within a few feet of deer and bear. Sometimes my city friends ask me what I do for entertainment in the wilderness without TV or all the urban activities. There is usually sort of a blank stare when I say that I like to walk in the woods.

Are you wondering why these encounters with the animal powers are important to me? To people who accept magic into their world, these special events are signs of power. For magic to come into our lives, we have only to recognize and celebrate magic. Denying magic and seeing the world as a series of accidents and coincidences is every human's right, however for me, a world without magic would be unbearably boring.

Hummingbirds are called flower eagles or seven arrows — medicine bird of the little people of the mountains. They have often come to me during ceremonies and a hummingbird feather was needed for my medicine bundle. On my first day of creating art in my newly-built studio, a hummingbird flew into my room. The little flower eagle banged against the window, and fearing she would be injured, I took her in my hands and carried her outside. Returning to the studio, after giving the flower eagle a prayer to take to Mother Nature, I discovered her beautiful give-away: five feathers left by the window. These feathers were made into a fan. Her gift is now a powerful tool in healing and conjuring ceremonies.

During another ceremony, an apprentice and myself were offering tobacco in our pipes while we sat by a stream. The hummingbirds kept blessing us by flying nearby. For years I had sought after a name for my medicine pipe. The name "Flower Eagle" came into my mind at the exact instant a hummingbird hovered four inches from my nose, with direct eye-to-eye contact. She then flew around my head, touching my hair with her wings. Next, the flower eagle flew to my apprentice, touching her head.

As my sacred pipe was lifted and her new name given to the universe, a hawk flew down the canyon wall behind us. The little eagle swooped and came up with a snake in its claws. It looked like the hawk was holding lightning, as the sun danced on the undulating snake. Quetzalcoatl [the Flying Serpent], an ancient teacher of the Mayan people, honored this naming.

When I encounter an animal, I honor the meeting and then try to see what sign or meaning the animal power is bringing to me. If I am in ceremony it may be especially meaningful, however any Sweet Medicine gift may be an important sign. I check back to what I was thinking at the exact time of the meeting or what my intent was when I started on a walk or the original purpose of the ceremony. In this way I have opened another way that the Earth Mother may speak to me. I enjoy the beauty of all of Nature's creatures, moreover, I celebrate the help that she gives to me through the animal powers.

BUFFALO SHIELD

When a herd of buffalo are attacked by predators, the adults form a protective circle with horns facing outward around the young calves. When the native peoples saw this, they called buffalos the "keepers of the circle." They knew that everything has a place on the medicine wheel of the universe; and within this one great circle there are many wheels that help us to understand life.

Two eagles, the feminine eagle of the west and the masculine eagle of the east, celebrate the buffalo's place on the wheel. The "Buffalo Shield" was made for a medicine brother who is a Sikh and on the reverse side is Aid Shakti, the mystical symbol of infinity.

(24 k gold, silver electrum, sugilite, turquoise,
lapis lazuli, pipestone, ivory, 1993)

JAGUAR PYRAMID

To the Mayans, it is the jaguar who dances around the north star in the constellation of the Big Dipper. The jaguar can easily be seen in what the people of the East named Ursa Major, spotted with stars, curving its long tail. Jaguar connects the power of the earth with the power of the stars. The medicine of the jaguar is the keeper of the balance of memory, within the movement of past, present, and future. The jaguar priestesses and priests knew the science of sacred numbers, astronomy, tribal histories and were responsible for the teaching of the people. Through their knowledge, these medicine people brought the Mayan civilization to a peak of power and culture — art, learning and harmony flourished.

Later, during a time of decline, the teachings became tools to enslave and control the people for the benefit of an elite few. Then, for a time, the jaguar became a symbol of fear and human sacrifice.

This power is special to me for jaguar is my personal medicine animal. The powers of the jaguar are reflected in my approach to art by the way that ancient cultures speak through my jewelry and sculpture. Jaguar is also a teacher to me in my search for balance.

(24 k gold, silver, azurite, turquoise, lapis lazuli,
coral, ivory, jet, sugilite, 1985)

WHITE OTTER SHIELD

Otter is known as the "playful one," who knows all the streams and rivers. They are a strong helper to medicine healers, for the otters teach the healing of waters, and through this, the circulatory systems of the body. My sundance chief has his patients hold on to an otter hide when he doctors them in the ceremony. On the reverse side of this shield is the lightning spirit of the otter.

(Silver, carved ivory, turquoise, lapis lazuli, 1985)

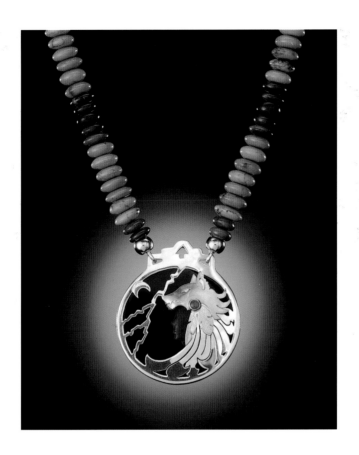

WOLF SHAMAN

Wolf is the path finder who knows all the trails of the world. From this power, wolf is the medicine animal of teachers who help us to find a path to follow in our live's journey. A teacher is not always a human; we can connect with our inner teacher, a power from the world of Nature, or even a wolf.

One of my favorite books is Never Cry Wolf *by Farley Mowat. In this true story, Farley is a scientist sent by the government to study wolves because they are believed to be responsible for the disappearance of the caribou. His time alone with the wolves becomes a visionquest in which he discovers that wolf is his animal power. Also, wolf teaches Farley that they are an important part of the balance of Nature and actually help the caribou herds to stay healthy.*

(24k gold, electrum, silver, pipestone, black onyx, turquoise, malachite, sugilite, emerald, 1993)

CRYSTAL EAGLE

Crystals have been used throughout history as healing stones. They vibrate at a very constant rate that enables us to use this power in making radios, watches, and computers. Shamanistic doctors use this energy within the crystals to intensify the healing process. Quartz crystals can be placed on the body to balance and open the energy field that surrounds us. The crystals assist the patient in being more receptive, so the shaman is more able to use the healing arts within her or his discipline.

The "Crystal Eagle" that is set into this shield was chipped by a Canadian Ojibway in the same way arrowheads are chipped, by striking them with a deer antler. Like the immense power within the crystal beings, this eagle is the Thunderbird, whose voice is thunder and whose eyes flash lightning.

(24 k gold, silver, turquoise, quartz crystal, rubies, diamonds, 1983)

BLUE HERONS

One spring day I was walking along the creek that runs through our land in the early morning. My quiet meditations were shattered by a primordial scream as what appeared to be an extinct pterodactyl flew out from the brush near my feet. After swallowing my heart back to its normal position in my anatomy, I marveled at the magnetism of the five foot high blue heron that had seemed a moment before to be twice my size. Soon after, a letter arrived from a medicine friend in Canada which read: "When you see a blue heron standing on both feet you are a person that knows truth." That same week I saw the blue heron standing by the lake and knew that I needed to honor this power with my art.

The need to make this jewelry piece was forgotten as, a few months later I was riding my Harley through the Canadian Rockies. It was the magical moment of twilight and I was thrilled to see an eagle sitting in her nest by the lake as a blue heron took flight from the bank of the lake and passed in front of me twenty feet in the air. A silvery transparent mystical curtain descended from the heron and hung suspended across the road as I rode my bike through it. As I tried to understand this cosmic event, I noticed that my bright red motorcycle and my black leathers were covered with heron droppings. Upon returning home, I promptly started work on the heron piece.

(24 k gold, electrum, silver, 22 k gold,
aqua marine, rainbow moonstones, 1991.
In the collection of Olivia and George Harrison.)

FREYA

In Northern Europe, the leader of the Divine Grandmothers, or Primal Matriarchs, is the Great Goddess Freya. She is the ruling ancestress of the elder gods, teacher of Odin in the arts of magic and divine power.

Frey is the twin brother of Freya, god of Yule, the "pagan" (which means the way of the people of the land) festival at Winter Solstice. As the shortest day ends and the days become longer, he is born of the virgin-sister-mother-bride.

The fifth day of our week is named in her honor. Freya is associated with love, and it is still considered auspicious by some to be married on Friday (Freya's Day).

(24 k gold, silver, electrum, black onyx, emerald, ivory, 1985)

(Reverse)

First Father   Sacred Twins of Creation   First Mother

SACRED TWINS OF CREATION

Touching love

Earth has called us to her so we may learn — love is her most sacred lesson

To feel an opening in the center where love is set free

To celebrate

The pains of love

The beauty of love

The learning of love

There is a touching that awakens the Sacred Twins in oneself

The union of self that is necessary

For love

For life

For joy

Sacred Goddess / Sacred God, we honor this gift, transcending expectations so that we may know the fullness of giving love

In this magical place — powers of spirit will expand, art will blossom, new understanding will be found

Jump into the abyss

Knowing it is possible to fall, to soar with wings

Awaking each morning

To celebrate that there is another day to love

Within the moment of bliss we touch the wholeness of self

In this instant we are no longer a lonely child

There is a knowing

We can become all of creation

Touching love

(Bronze, 16 inches, 1989, limited edition of 25)

SACRED BALANCE
THE FEMININE POWERS

CHAPTER 11

People have said that my art work seems overbalanced toward feminism and the celebration of the Goddess. To me, most of the world has demonstrated an imbalance in the direction of patriarchy for so long that to bring about balance I must lean toward Goddess at this time. If matriarchy was the predominant force in the world and reflected an imbalance, I would be stressing masculinism. The ambition of my work is to embrace the balance of both genders and all races. My wish is to create an artistic expression that celebrates all the differences that our world family brings to the wheel of life, imaging no limitations on realizing our full potential.

During the age of the Goddess, the Earth was seen as sacred, however many of the patriarchal tribes that came into dominance later tried to discredit the spiritual power of the Earth Mother Goddess. The Goddess was removed from our mythology by the leaders of the "new" religions to try to eliminate ancestral spiritual practices. Also, the Goddess was hidden for political reasons in order to control certain groups, races and genders of our human family.

The way of balance is still embraced by many of the world's peoples including the Native Americans who celebrate the balance of the Goddess and the God. In their prayers, indigenous peoples speak to both Mother Earth and Great Spirit.

In studying the ancient history of humanity I realized that there was much to learn from her story. The removal of the Great Goddess in all her aspects had left a void in our mythological life. I realized that the consequence of the resulting imbalance has been disastrous on our environment. The Earth is no longer seen as our Mother, she is seen as a resource to exploit. Many people seem to view the Earth as an enemy instead of the nurturing power that she is. To our ancient grandparents, harming the Earth would be as great a crime as harming their own maternal mother. The loss of the Goddess has caused imbalance in our environment, our communities, our families and ourselves.

Some of the things that I learned from reading feminist literature were shocking to me. How in many parts of the world women are still seen as property to be totally controlled by the men in their lives. In the recent history of my own country the "rule of thumb" law was considered humane treatment of a wife. The law was thought to protect women by saying that when a man beat his wife, he could only use a stick as large as his thumb. Laws like this make me wonder what life was like for my grandmother or what effects the gender biases still cause in our world.

As artists, we may strive to heal imbalances like this in the mythology of our present time as we look to our current myths and see what aspects we have lost. If I use the image of the Goddess often in my work, it is because I see her being neglected in many ways. The Venus archetype, the sexual goddess of love is definitely alive in our culture. This archetype was allowed to prosper because it served the interests of the emerging patriarchy in historical times. We have only to view our films, advertising and stereotypes to see this image of woman in our culture. Hestia, goddess of the hearth, is still encouraged in our society with the way our nurturing mothers are honored in the world of today. There are several aspects of the Goddess missing today that were repressed and have left an imbalance in our lives. The wise woman or goddesses of wisdom like Athena, Sophia, Isis and other manifestations are hard to find in our modern myths. Kali the goddess of life and death is absent from our current mythology and may account for our denial and fear of the cycle of death and rebirth.

In my view of the world, I see that women and men enter the wheel of life from opposite sides and both are meant to learn about the whole circle. As we move around the wheel of life's lessons, each aspect of humanity is important and necessary. If the genders are divided down the middle and not allowed to experience the other side then, we may realize only one-half of our potential.

As I held my babies in my arms, I became a nurturer and resented any structural beliefs that try to keep me from this so-called feminine trait. Women may be naturally sensitive to nurturing, however the man that fails to develop that part of himself is missing a wonderful gift of life. Women hold within their bodies the potential to create life and they are closer to manifestation from the source of Nature. This creative resource makes it natural for women to be in touch with the intuitive power needed in the creating of magic. Although it is more difficult for men to be intuitive, we are denying much of our power if we as men fail to celebrate our intuition.

The direction from which we enter the medicine wheel of life is not meant to limit our potential. Men are said to be more in touch with the mind and women are seen as being more influenced by the emotional body. This has led to other biases that often honor our grandfathers more as teachers than our grandmothers and women are expected to be more in touch with their feelings. Some of my greatest teachers have been the wise women in my life and anyone who does not go to their grandmothers for instruction is missing one of life's treasures. Also many of our problems as men result from trying to live life cut off from our emotions because we were taught that it was not manly to be connected to our feelings.

The limitations that we think we have are really our greatest opportunities for they point the way to expansion as we enter into a greater fullness of who we are. We may see the direction that we need to expand into, if we can feel the limitations imposed by our culture and our life's traumas. Many of the world's peoples see our life's journey as moving around the wheel in a spiral that takes us to the center. When I am spiraling to the center of the medicine wheel, I am able to celebrate my maleness while honoring my feminine powers on my path toward wholeness. As I get closer to the center of the wheel, I know that my art work will reflect to the outer world that which is happening in my inner world. My art work becomes a self-teacher because it is a mirror, reflecting my life's processes and passages.

If I see my work as a tool for healing the imbalances that I see in the world the art pieces may have a larger circle of influence. The first place to start the healing process is with myself. When I find the places in myself that are out of harmony, I may find ways to call balancing archetypes into my life and into my art. When I view the world's problems around me, I feel the necessity to awaken the healing powers in my work that are necessary to bring equilibrium .

The Native Americans work with a council wheel that is helpful in looking at the different archetypal powers as we move clockwise around the eight directions of the wheel. Starting in the east there is the heyoka and the artist. Next come the peace chiefs and then in the south are the war chiefs. The medicine people and healers are in the southwest and then the powers of woman are in the west. As we move around the circle the council of law is in the northwest; in the north the hunters and workers; and in the northeast are the people responsible for enforcing the laws called the dog soldiers. When a law is talked about it starts in the east and each person speaks in turn for the power of the direction where they sit and how it can affect the proposed law. The balance of this wheel was worked out over thousands of years in ways that are sometimes obvious and sometimes subtle.

It shows wisdom that the peace chiefs speak before the war chiefs and then the healers and so on... As each direction speaks on how a new law will effect a particular power, each direction also talks concerning the law that is in the center of the wheel: how the law will affect the children. The last person to speak is the dog soldier who is responsible for protecting the children. We may feel more comfortable speaking from the part of the wheel that is our personal expertise, however we need to learn to move around the wheel to become a whole human.

If we see our self as being the council wheel, then we may have a way to look at our personal powers. How functional is the part of us that holds our powers of woman sitting in the west? These powers include nurturing, intuition, dreaming, ... and in the southwest have we learned to touch ourselves and others in a healing way? Do we have a good worker and are we able to embrace peace and war?

When I find a place on the wheel that is out of balance in myself or in the community around me, then I may embrace an archetypal power that speaks for this direction in my life and in my art. As I work toward wholeness within myself, then the world around me will become more in harmony. The world's problems seem so overwhelming to me that I as an individual seem insignificant. Yet, I feel that if only a small percentage of us can find a personal equilibrium, then there may be a shift in all of humanity toward the sacred balance.

Kawhu

In the Kachina ceremonies of the Zuni and Hopi tribes, Kawhu is the Eagle Being. To both the Europeans and to the Native Americans, the eagle is the symbol associated with spirit, lightning, thunder and fire. People all over the Earth work in a sacred way with this archetype in their ceremonies and in their dreams. We have all known that freedom of spirit as we fly in our dreaming state.

When in ceremony with the Eagle Kachina, the ceremonial dancer merges with this power. The Kachinas can then teach and heal the people included in the ceremony. Having relationship with the spirit world in this way is to experience Kawhu.

(24 k gold, electrum, silver, pipestone, lapis lazuli,
black onyx, ivory, quartz, malachite, 1984, first award, Indian Market,
Santa Fe. In the collection of Michael Jackson.)

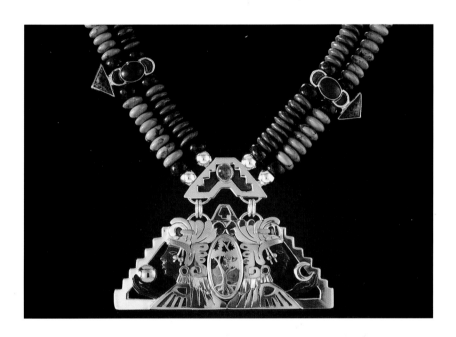

Sacred Twins

Tezcatlipoca is the jaguar deity, the smoking mirror, keeper of the night sky and wizard of astronomy. Quetzalcoatl is the plumed serpent, keeper of the day sky and the fire-bringer. Together, the two Mayan deities kindled the first fire of creation. Tezcatlipoca is called storm-bringer and is sacred to the moon and stars. Quetzalcoatl is called gift-bringer, sacred to the sun.

The forked sundance tree of life between the twins again refers to the sacred balance. The two limbs of the sundance tree are medicine mirrors, one side reflecting the other. Life/death, day/night, woman/man owe their existence to the mirroring of their opposites. While dancing to the forked tree, I was, for a while, able to step outside the world of duality and see that we are all one.

(24 k gold, silver, pipestone, malachite, emerald,
sugilite, turquoise,azurite, 1993)

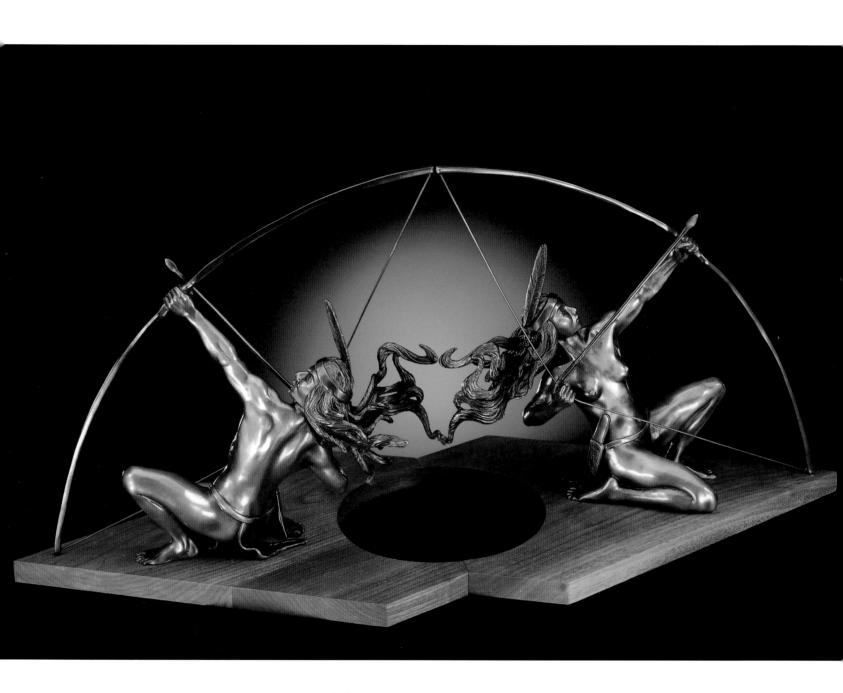

WARROIRS OF THE RAINBOW

(Bronze, 13 inches, 1991, limited edition of 40)

WARRIORS OF THE RAINBOW
THE PROPHECY

There are many ancient prophesies among the Native American peoples concerning the times in which we are living. The indigenous tribes were not surprised when the black, white, and yellow peoples arrived on their shores, because their prophets had spoken of the coming of other races. They knew that the new tribes would overwhelm the ancient cultures of the land they called Turtle Island, until the spirit of the Indian would almost disappear.

In our time, the spirit of the Indians will be born anew into all of the races that have gathered in this land. A portion of each of the different races of the rainbow colors will see that we are all one family. They are called the "Warriors of the Rainbow."

This new community of mixed races and cultures will recognize that other humans are all their relations. The Rainbow People are not called warrioresses and warriors because they are waging war on other tribes, rather they are making war on the parts of themselves and their culture that are out of balance. In discovering the balance of the self, they will find harmony with all life. The Warriors of the Rainbow will bring with them a new time of living in harmony with our environment and with all peoples.

It was in the mid-sixties and I was living alone at the Garden of Spring when I first learned about the Indian prophesies. These traditional stories spoke strongly to me because I felt so out of place with the world of my youth. As my friends and I experimented with different tribal ways of living, we were creating a style of life that seemed to fit in with the prophetic tales.

At that time I was actively involved in the peace movement of the sixties therefore I had trouble calling myself a warrior. Over the years I have become more comfortable with seeing myself and the people in my circle as warrioresses and warriors. I began to see that a warrior is not necessarily someone who goes out to slaughter and kill, there is also the spiritual warrior.

The heros and sheros of our mythological legends typically go out on an adventure, slay a monster and then return a more powerful person. Very often the adversaries in the sagas referred to the monsters that are a part of our self. The conditioning of our society, our traumas and our personal desires often conflict with what is best for our higher good. The historical warrior who was an excellent killer in the end is often not seen as significant as the warrior who fought his/her battles within the self, received a greater understanding about the universe and then returned to give away to the people by teaching.

The warriors who are fighting exterior battles are often distracting themselves from the far more fearful war of inner work. I have seen people confront excruciatingly painful parts of their inner self and to me they are often more courageous than many of our veterans of war. The great generals of history who conquered territory and created empires are to me not as consequential as our spiritual teachers who have shown us how to live in balance. The Buddha, the Christ, Isis, Krishna, Kwai-Yin, White Buffalo Woman and all of our other spiritual teachers have taken the heroic journey into the center of their being to bring back the wisdom that they then gifted to us. As warriors and warrioresses of the rainbow they have left us many paths that will lead us to the place where we can become our full potential. If these prophesies elicit a feeling in you, then you are possibly a member of this tribe of the rainbow races and I celebrate you as a part of our ever-growing family.

WARRIORS
SCULPTURE

I have wanted to honor the Warriors of the Rainbow in an art piece for over two decades while the image and the understanding grew stronger in me. The archetypal image of the warrioress is very neglected in our culture so I knew that I needed to create the sculpture to help heal this imbalance. In historical times the powerful warrioress goddess was an important part of the way we viewed life. Artemis, Diana, the Amazon warrioresses, Osa, Pele and many other goddesses radiated dynamic forceful action. In my sculpture I wanted to embody the energy of these ancient goddesses.

When the drawing was finally started I saw that the two bows would form the arc of the rainbow. As the wind blown hair was drawn, a buffalo skull appeared in the negative space between the two figures. One of the buffalo's medicine powers is the keeper of the wheel of life so I felt that this energy wanted to come to the piece.

The original sculpture was molded out of plasticine, a soft oil-based clay that would not harden over the long process that took several months.

The warrioress was created first and then a mold was taken of the finished plasticine piece. The warrioress was then transformed into the warrior by adding to and taking away the clay. It was very magical to see the sculpture take life and the two figures felt truly balanced as they emanated one power.

Over the years, I have watched the lives of several of my contemporaries who were in art school with me. Some of my friends who were the most artistically gifted students have chosen not to produce their artistic visions. Although some of them could draw better than I, there was something missing to fan their spark of creative energy into a blazing fire. I feel that what is missing has a lot to do with the warrioress/warrior part of us.

I have often wondered what happened to me to move my life into such a different direction. While in college, I started to notice that when my friends wanted me to smoke a big one with them and lie on the beach, I had to stay in my studio and work. Sometimes I would work through the night and I was often exhausted and stressed. Creating art became my primary focus in life even when my artistic passion was detrimental to my health or to my relationships.

It may have been that I was jolted into another way of viewing life when a close friend of mine was killed by a car as we were motorcycling through Europe. Around that time, I started to see my art not as a way to attract attention to myself, rather I saw that my art work might be a beneficial gift to the world. The spiritual warrioress/warrior somehow comes to a place where they need to give-away to something that is greater than themselves. This shift in vision was for me the turning point in my becoming a Warrior of the Rainbow.

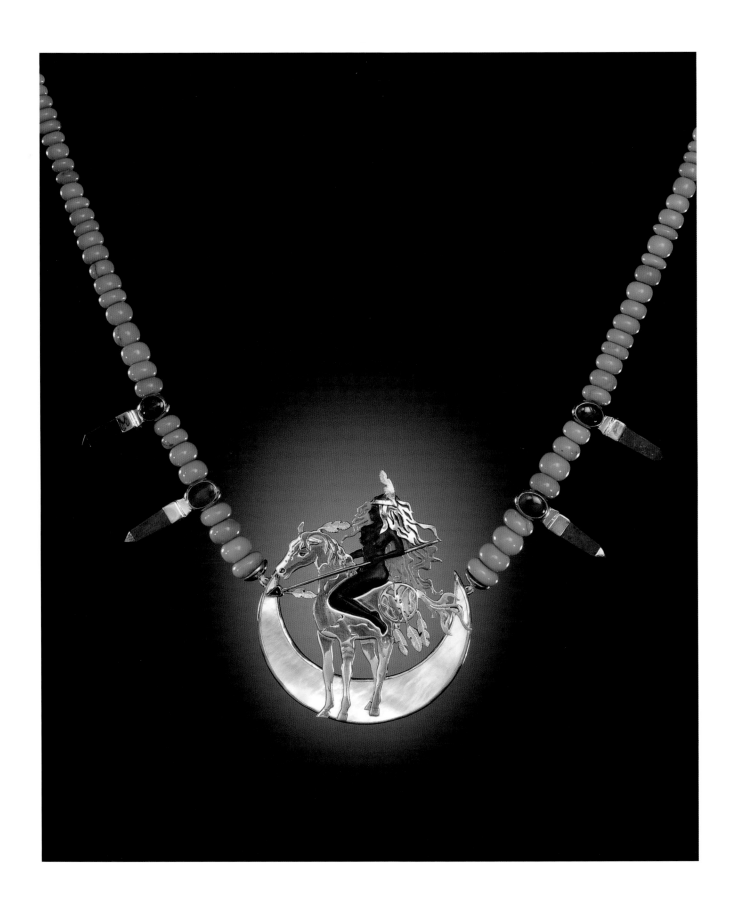

WARRIORESS

In ancient times the Goddess was celebrated in all of her aspects: the Virgin , Mother and Crone. She has the potential for creating life, life giver and life taker. Seeing the Goddess in all her aspects gives us a way of touching all of these parts in ourselves.

In more recent times, we have been taught to believe that women should disown parts of themselves. One of these aspects is her warrioress. The way this has been accomplished is by writing this more aggressive feminine archetype out of our histories, art and literature. Heroes abound, however seldom do we see the shero.

The stories of the Amazon tribes and how their women were distinguished in the art of war are still found in our literature. The Greeks especially respected and feared the Amazon warrioresses. They told tales of how the womens' magic battle-cries could render their enemies defenseless. The name Amazon means "moon-woman" and they belonged to matriarchal tribes that worshiped the Goddess. They fought furiously against the patriarchal tribes that were overwhelming the world.

To make warring and aggressiveness the ruling power in life is not the purpose in honoring the warrioress or warrior. By integrating this part of ourselves we can bring it into balance. In honoring the warrioress/warrior we can fight effectively for truth, compassion, wisdom and healing when we encounter problems in our self and in our world.

In her book Red Feather, Joan Grant remembers a time in Native American history when the warrioress was honored. This story was the inspiration for the "Warrioress" necklace. She is prepared for battle and there is war paint on her horse. The three lines on the front leg mean that she has "counted coup" or touched her enemies three times in combat and the hoof-print on the back leg means that she stole her horse.

(24 k gold, electrum, silver, copper, ruby,
carved pipestone, sugilite, lapis lazuli, turquoise, 1990)

Diana (The Huntress)

The Queen of Heaven, Sacred Huntress, is called Artemis by the Grecians, and by the Romans, Diana. She is the Triple Goddess; Lunar Virgin, Mother of all Creatures and the Huntress (destroyer). Diana is also called "Diana of the Grove" and she is celebrated within the sacred groves. The priests of Diana are known as King of the Wood or the King Stag.

Contemporary culture seems to be uncomfortable with goddesses that are also warrioresses. In fact the word warrioress is not even in my computer's spell check or my dictionary. The image in our mythology, passed down to us by most historians is of the Goddess as the fertility and mother aspect of womankind. In Diana, her more dynamic aspect as the Huntress has survived. She retains her rightful role as the Great Goddess, embodiment of strength and power — swift, straight and deadly as her arrows.

(24k gold, silver, electrum, carved pipestone, moonstone,
emerald, malachite, crystal, diamond, 1986)

VESTA / EGERIA

Diana, the Huntress, is also celebrated as Egeria, the elemental goddess of the springs who blesses women and children and aids in childbirth. Often within Diana's groves there is a sacred spring dedicated to Egeria, who succors women who bring their burdens to her.

The hearth goddess, Vesta is another aspect of Diana. Within her temples, the vestal priestesses tended the holy, generative fire of the Earth Mother Creatress. This sacred fire upon her alter was kept burning continuously in honor of the Great Goddess. Once a year all the fires in the village were extinguished. In a ceremony, fire was taken from Vesta's altar to each house so that the household hearths would share Vesta's sacred fire.

The two elemental goddesses in this necklace are holding fire and water to celebrate these aspects of Diana.

(24 k gold, silver, electrum, emerald, tourmaline, crystal, 1988)

TEMPLE DOORS

(Bronze, 27 inches, 1984, limited edition of 25)

SWEET MEDICINE / TEMPLE DOORS

Egyptian art had been a great influence in my work for several years at the time that I viewed the "treasures of Tutankamun." Since my Egyptian-styled jewelry was featured in the museum shop, I was allowed to wander alone through what became the most attended art show in history. The pieces that I was very familiar with from my Egyptian art books were now experienced first hand.

The room in which the pieces were displayed, felt almost like it had been transformed into a temple. I approached the objects in the show with a reverence that is given sacred art whenever I encounter it. The gold mask of Tutankamun left an especially strong impression on me. It was not a portrait of the Egyptian king, it depicted the king as his transcendent potential for deity.

Melting together all of my gold, I made it into a huge sheet to make a gold mask set with lapis lazuli. My vision was a self-portrait in the opulent and transcendent tradition of the wonderful mask in this show. About this time the world market cost of gold increased about 800% from my original purchase price. Regretfully, I had to use my sheet of gold to be made into jewelry in order to support my family.

Years later when I was working on a bronze sculpture, I realized that if bronze is polished as in my jewelry making process, it would be very much like gold. As I designed the mask, I realized that if I was sculpting the transcendent aspect of myself that there needed to be two pieces in order to celebrate the female and male balance of the Sacred Twins.

Into the two pieces I wove the oral traditions that spoke concerning the origins of the sundance teachings that I learned from the peoples of the American plains. After the submergence of the Atlantean Islands in the Atlantic Ocean there were many migrations of the displaced tribes. The Sweet Medicine sundance teaching of the sea tribes was brought to the Great Plains area of Turtle Island. There was also a migration of tribes from the Mayan cities to the south. The Mayan peoples were led by a woman chief named Temple Doors who added the teachings of the medicine wheel to the Sweet Medicine Sundance.

(Bronze, 27 inches, 1984, limited edition of 25)

SWEET MEDICINE

(Bronze, 27 inches, 1984, limited edition of 25)

SACRED ART SACRED EARTH

There are many paths that lead toward the center of understanding that is ourselves and the path that I have chosen to honor is sacred art. Reflecting our culture and our innermost self, art is a universal language. As dancers, painters, musicians, sculptors, writers, ... we seem to have a way to express our inner and outer world.

As I continue to find balance within my personal circle and the greater circle of my community I may see it reflected in my work. The archetypal powers that work toward a balance can come through my work to create more harmony in my life and community.

My inspirations are rooted in the traditions and myths of our global family. The natural balance of Nature and the interrelationship of all her creatures and powers are my greatest teachers. As I learn to honor the relationship and interdependence I share with Nature, the magic of the sacred becomes reflected in my art.

I feel that artists have a sacred duty when they work with the archetypes or magical symbols. The archetypical symbols are our personal mythology that help us to touch and understand the conflicts and harmonies of the different parts of ourselves. The personal myths that appear in our art work also speak to a remembrance in all humankind. These powerful symbols can be used to exploit people or to heal them by helping to restore balance with all the powers within the self.

The use of archetypal symbols is no longer considered a sacred responsibility. Most often, these symbols are used to sell products, manipulate people or control their minds. As artists, we have a sacred duty when we bring back the archetypal image from the void. The powers we bring into our work may help people to connect with their inner teacher, healer or protector. Sometimes, that which we bring back from the void, encircles others with the awe and reverence of life.

In my journey through life as an artist and as a medicine person, I have come to understand that in order to create sacred art I need to love and celebrate the Earth as sacred. When power and healing is manifested within my work I feel that it comes not from me, simply through me from the Heavens and from the Earth. My wish is to make every step I take upon the land a prayer to the Earth. As the Earth heals me and teaches me balance, then healing and balance can touch other people through my work.

Now, in my mid years, I look back on my life and see that I have lived an equal amount of time in the natural areas of our land and our great urban centers. Both are a part of the experience that life has gifted to me. When I leave my forest home, I find it difficult to drive in a Los Angeles traffic jam — late for an appointment. Staying in my peaceful mountain wilderness never to return to a city is sometimes a very attractive idea to me. In my heart, I know that to stop frequenting our cities would be to cut me off from the majority of our human family and therefore I would be cutting off part of myself.

As I live close to the natural rhythms of Nature, the power of the Earth is absorbed into my work. My relations in our cities will be able to feel the force of these natural rhythms in my work and touch the land where I live. In that touching they may know a little of the healing that the Earth has brought to my life.

When speaking of our relationship to Nature, one of our Northwest grandfathers has created some of the most beautiful prose I have ever experienced. I want to include it in this book because it says much of what I have been trying to say to you in a more wise and eloquent manner. These are the words of Chief Seattle in answer to President Franklin Pierce when he stated that he wanted to buy the tribal land where the Chief's people lived.

"How can you buy or sell the sky? The land? The idea is strange to us. If we do not own the freshness of the air and the sparkle of the water, how can you buy them? Every part of this Earth is sacred to my people. Every shining pine needle, every sandy shore, every mist in the dark woods, every meadow, every humming insect. All are holy in the memory and experience of my people.

If we sell you our land, remember that the air is precious to us, that the air shares its spirit with all the life it supports. The wind that gave our grandfather his first breath also received his last sigh. The wind also gives our children the spirit of life. So if we sell you our land, you must keep it apart and sacred, a place where man can go to taste the wind that is sweetened by the meadow flowers.

Will you teach your children what we have taught our children? That the Earth is our Mother? What befalls the Earth befalls all the sons of the Earth.

This we know: The Earth does not belong to man, man belongs to the Earth. All things are connected like the blood that unites us all. Man did not weave the web of life, he is merely a strand in it. Whatever he does to the web, he does to himself.

We are part of the Earth and She is part of us. The perfumed flowers are our sisters, the bear, the deer, the great eagle, these are our brothers. The rivers are our brothers, they carry our canoes and feed our children. Each ghostly reflection in the clear water of the lakes tells of events in the memories of my people. The water's murmurs are the voice of my father's father.

We love this Earth as a newborn loves its mother's heartbeat. So if we sell you our land, love it as we have loved it. Care for it as we have cared for it. Hold in your mind a memory of the land as it is when you receive it. Preserve the land for all children and love it as God loves us all.

One thing we know: There is only one God. No man be he red or white can be apart. We are brothers after all."

Like our great chief, I have learned that the land and I are one. The universe has gifted me with life and has bequeathed to me the Earth, to be my mother. In celebrating all the gifts from the Creatress/Creator I have worked with my ceremonies and my art to give back the Earth, her peoples, and her future generations. Dancing with the archetypal messengers of the universe, I will keep my feet connected to the earth. As an artist, I know that if I can embrace the wholeness of existence, then every art work I do will be a ceremony to the "Sacred Earth" and the pieces will mirror life as "Sacred Art."

ALL MY RELATIONS

YEMAYA

The Ocean Mother is called Yemaya by the Caribbean Island peoples. She traveled to the New World when her people were enslaved and taken from Western Africa. She is called different names by the various tribes of the world and her power reaches up the great rivers where offerings and prayers are given to her. She is bringer of abundance and prosperity and Yemaya is honored with similar ceremonies from Brazil to Indonesia. At the Summer Solstice, offerings of food, flowers and gifts are put on small decorated boats and then launched into the Sea.

The tribal peoples understand that she is the womb of creation and that life was first generated within her waters. The gift of life and all the abundance that she provides for the humans is honored by the sacrifice of the offerings. In most modern cultures it seems that we take from her to the point of upsetting her delicate balance and then thank her with offerings of our sewage, garbage, and industrial pollution.

My Western African brother Malidoma Somé and the people of his tribe, the Dagara, worship her by the name Mammy Wata. She is sometimes seen in the ocean or river as a mermaid . Last summer he and his wife Sobonfu were visiting here during the Summer Solstice and we did a ceremony to the Ocean Mother. I had just finished the Yemaya necklace and a drawing of the piece was put on the sail of our give-away boat. We all felt like the spring of abundance flowing from her source was tied up and a prosperity ceremony was needed. With ceremony, the little boat of offerings was given to the river and she received it into her womb. With the completion of this book and the publication of Malidoma's books, Ritual, *and* Of Water and The Spirit, *the past year has been very abundant for us.*

(22 k gold, 24 k gold, electrum, emerald, pipestone,
turquoise, sugilite, lapis lazuli, 1992)

LIST OF PLATES